Getting to know you –

Great Words of the Faith

C.Brian Ross

Vol 1 in the "Getting to know you" series

By the same author:

Foundations of the Faith *(vol.2 in the "Getting to know you … " series)*

Defending the Faith *(vol.3 in the "Getting to know you … " series)*

All Scripture quotations, unless otherwise indicated, are taken from the Revised Standard Version of the Bible, ©1952 [2nd edition, 1971] by the Division of Christian Education of the National Council of the Churches of Christ in the United States of America. Used by permission. All rights reserved.

This was the version that I used most frequently when the original short series of messages was being prepared.

All rights reserved. No part of this publication may be reproduced, stored in a retrieval system, or transmitted, in any form or by any means,
electronic, mechanical, photocopying, recording, or otherwise, without the prior written permission of the author.

ISBN-13: 978-1540613547

ISBN-10: 1540613542

© Copyright 2012.

Also available as an e-book
ASIN: B009EG6TJW
at
https://www.amazon.co.uk/dp/B009EG6TJW

Twenty-five chapters and twenty-four Great Bible Words. Love, naturally, deserves two chapters. Brian Ross has preached on many of these themes, but the book puts him in your home, talking by the fireside. He has read widely, and has many stories to tell. It is homely theology with notes of exhortation and encouragement. I especially liked his common sense approach to holiness and his link between righteousness and social action. Full of quotable sayings, and supremely centred on Jesus Christ.

Rev. Dr. Derek Cook
Evangelist; Founder of *Christians in the Dordogne*

Brian presents his work as the long-term fruit of preaching and broadcasting. His aim is to give simple explanations of key Christian terms for the 'ordinary Joe' who has no formal theological training, but who would benefit from a clearer grasp of basic Christian concepts. He maintains a preaching style throughout, and illustrates his explanations from his own rich experience and wide reading. Throughout the work, he challenges the reader to respond to his writing.

Rev. Dr. George J. Mitchell
Former Lecturer in Old Testament Studies, the Bible Training Institute, Glasgow

There are two kinds of simplicity: one on this side of complexity, and one on the other. In Great Words of the Faith, Brian Ross writes with simplicity on the right side of complexity. In so doing he enables us to understand difficult Christian terminology. Well done Brian! In simplicity lies beauty - something our minds can't resist.

Rev. Dr. Lawson Murray
President - Scripture Union Canada.

Introduction

Getting to know you –

Great Words of the Christian Faith

This book started its life some thirty years before it was written! It began as a series of messages preached before the congregation of Bellshill: St.Andrew's Parish Church at the evening teaching service of worship. Some twenty years later, those same messages became the focus of a series of radio broadcasts that I presented on the Christian radio station, Revival FM. Then, just a few years after that, I revised some of the messages again, and preached them before the two parts of the congregation of Calderhead Erskine Parish Church, in Shotts and in Allanton.

Only after all of that, have I 'taken the plunge' in putting these thoughts together as a book with a considerable amount of additional material. It is my hope that, having commenced as preached messages to an ordinary group of ordinary people – and not as a series of lectures to a class of Bible College students – they will still be understood by ordinary people who, while using many of these words, are not always clear as to their meanings! They are words that can flow so easily from the lips of pastors, ministers, and theologians, but that may be totally meaningless to the 'average' member of the congregation! Some of them are words that we may use 'in church', but that we would never dream of using in our everyday conversations with our families, our friends, or our colleagues in either work or recreation. However, just as we need to have some grasp of the specialised vocabulary in any subject, if we are going to understand it, we need to have some idea as to what these words mean if we are going to understand some of the great themes of the Christian Gospel more fully.

As a preacher, rather than an author, I have endeavoured to maintain a 'preaching style' even in my writing. However, as a lover of the English language, I have also endeavoured not to fall into too 'chatty' a style that would do injustice to the written word.

Thanks is due to many people. It was sitting under the ministry of the late Rev. George B. Duncan of St.George's-Tron Parish Church, Glasgow; and under the tutelage of the late Prof William Barclay of Trinity College, and the University of Glasgow; that taught me the importance, and the benefit, of using language that didn't require an Honours degree in Theology to be understood. I am grateful to many with whom, over the years, I have shared my own thinking, and who have helped to bring some element of clarity to it. It was Albert Einstein who said that "If you can't explain it simply, you don't understand it well enough." I hope that, in dealing with some very difficult concepts, I will have demonstrated that I do have some understanding!

Being a former student of the Bible Training Institute, Glasgow, gave me access to the Library in its descendant: the International Christian College. I am grateful that I had the opportunity to spend time there, in research.

I was delighted that the Rev. Dr. George Mitchell, formerly Lecturer in Old Testament Studies in The Bible Training Institute, Glasgow, read over my initial attempts, and offered some hints borne out of his own experience as an author. A new friend, Sgt Mark Milligan of Strathclyde Police, also agreed to read over my manuscript – from the point of view of one who claims to be an atheist. Their helpful comments have been greatly appreciated – but, of course, the final responsibility remains my own!

My dear wife, too, is worthy of so much of my thanks for her patience with me over many years, and her encouragement in all of the varied undertakings on which I have embarked.

However, my greatest thanks must go to the Lord Whom I have sought to serve, however imperfectly, over many, many, years. It is He Who has endowed me with any gifting that I might demonstrate; it is He Who has inspired me in the preparation of countless messages over the years; it is He Who granted me the full salvation that I enjoy; it is He Who has given me the great hope that I will spend eternity in His nearer presence. To Him, and to Him alone, be all the glory, and honour; majesty, and praise; world without end.

Motherwell, 2012

It wasn't easy to determine the order in which these words – each, to some extent, as great as any of the others – should appear. The original series of sermons had no pre-determined order and has, as already stated, been greatly expanded, but I have come up with the following that will, I trust, provide some rationale for the order followed in the book! Of course, not unexpectedly, there is overlapping, and intertwining with, and among, them all!

Faith, which is the Gift of God, leads to
Repentance,
Conversion, and
Salvation through the
Propitiation that ensured
Atonement, because I didn't
Procrastinate and, by the
Grace of God, I am
Redeemed. At that moment, I became a citizen of the
Kingdom of God, having been
Justified, made
Holy, covered with the
Righteousness of Jesus, and with the process of
Sanctification having commenced in me. I know that I have been
Predestined since before the beginning of time, and have a
Hope that is based on His
Covenant
Love, that will be with me until the
Rapture when, with the rest of the true
Church, I shall meet the second Persona of the
Trinity, my Lord
Jesus, "in the air", and
Worship Him throughout
Eternity.

Table of Contents

Faith	1
Repentance	11
Conversion	21
Salvation	33
Propitiation/Expiation	45
Atonement	55
Procrastination	63
Grace	69
Redemption	81
Kingdom of God	89
Justification	99
Holiness	109
Righteousness	119
Sanctification	131
Predestination	143
Hope	153
Covenant	163
Love	173
Love (a Case Study)	183
Rapture	193
Church	211
The Trinity	223
Jesus	233
Worship	241
Eternity	255

Chapter 1

FAITH

"The only thing that counts is faith, expressing itself through love." (Gal.5:6)

The title of this book is "Getting to know you – Great Words of the Faith". That faith is the Christian faith, and the word with which we commence is the word 'faith' itself. What is it? Why is it necessary? How is it obtained? These are the questions that we will be asking, and we will be seeking answers to them from God's own Word.

It has been claimed that "Faith is the great cop-out, the great excuse to evade the need to think and evaluate evidence. Faith is belief in spite of, even perhaps because of, the lack of evidence." (Richard Dawkins) However, such a comment displays a total misunderstanding of Biblical faith!

First of all, then, what is faith? Or, more correctly, "What is it that this word signifies? What do we mean when we speak about 'faith'?" Well, we may begin by noting what it's not, and we quickly discover that it's not a concrete substance. It isn't something tangible, with physical properties; it isn't the sort of thing that I can go into a shop and buy; it isn't something that may be weighed on a scale, or measured with a rule.

1

So that's what it's not! But what is it? What is faith? Well, there is a sense in which it is something that you and I, and even Richard Dawkins, exercise every day, and we do so in a variety of ways. When I board a bus, or a train, I have no absolute guarantee that the driver is qualified to drive; that he is in a fit state to drive; that his health is all that it needs to be in order to carry the responsibility of driving. However, I still board my chosen mode of transport! I am exercising a form of faith; I am acting in a specific manner even in the absence of 'concrete' proof that it is safe for me to do so.

Or I may visit a particular restaurant for lunch. I study the menu, and decide which dish I would prefer for each course. Now, I have no absolute guarantee that the chef knows what he is doing; or that the food has been maintained at the correct temperature; or that the kitchen staff are following the correct procedures with regard to hygiene. Nevertheless, when the dish is set before me, I tuck in quite happily. Once again, I am exercising a form of faith. I am placing my trust in another without any absolute guarantee that it is safe for me to do so! At that level, Richard Dawkins does have a valid point!

However, as indicated above, faith is something abstract. It is classed alongside justice, and truth, and mercy, and love. I may see and even, up to a point, be able to measure, the results of these things. But, of themselves, they are abstract, intangible, qualities. And Biblical faith – the faith that leads to salvation – is much, much more. It is

"... *the gift of God* ..." (Eph.2:8).

Biblical faith is not a sentimental wishfulness but a strong confidence in God and His Word, through Jesus Christ, Who is Himself

"... *the Author and Finisher of our faith*." (Heb.12:2).

The writer of that Letter to the Hebrew disciples of Jesus defined faith, for the believer, when he wrote that it is

> "... *the assurance of things hoped for; the conviction of things not seen.*" (Hebrews 11:1).

Two aspects of faith are noted by the inspired writer. He states, first of all, that faith is

> "... *the assurance of things hoped for;*"

Prof Barclay writes: "To the writer to the Hebrews, faith is a hope that is absolutely certain that what it believes is true, and that what it expects will come." (Daily Study Bible, *in loc*)

Christian faith has nothing to do with the hope of Charles Dickens' character, Mr Micawber. His constant 'hope' was that "something will turn up". But this is the hope that looks forward with wistful longing; not that which looks forward with absolute certainty.

> "... *the assurance of things hoped for;*"

However, the writer of this great letter to the early Hebrew disciples of Jesus also states that faith is

> "*the conviction of things not seen.*"

And here, the emphasis is that, even without anything in the way of outward evidence to support a belief in the promises of God, the man (or woman) of faith still retains a firm hold on them.

In the early days of the persecution of the followers of Jesus, a humble believer was brought before the judges. He told them that nothing that they could do could shake him because he believed that, if he was true to God, then God would be true to him. 'Do you really think', asked one of the judges, 'that the like of you will go to God and His glory?' 'I do not think', the man answered, 'I know!'

'I know' – absolute, utter conviction that what God has said is true. "God said it; I believe it; that's it; period!" The apostle Paul made the same proclamation of assurance –

> "*I know Whom I have believed ...*" (II Tim.1:12).

"*I know*"! And on such a basis is true faith built – a basis of absolute trust; of convinced certainty. Faith is the attitude whereby a man abandons all reliance on his own efforts to obtain salvation – whether it be by good works, or ethical goodness; membership of a congregation, or of an organisation; office in the church, or status in society; or anything else of which we might think. It is the attitude of complete trust in the Lord, Jesus the Christ; of reliance on Him alone for all that salvation means and entails.

When the Philippian jailer asked Paul and Silas,

> "*Sirs, what must I do to be saved?*",

they didn't present him with a list of rules and regulations; or an application form for membership. No! They answered, without any hesitation at all:

> "*Believe in the Lord Jesus Christ and you will be saved ...*" (Acts 16:31).

And the word translated '*Believe*' in English language versions is the word *pisteuson* – that comes from the root word *pistis* = faith! So the answer of Paul and Silas could quite legitimately be translated as "**Have faith** *in the Lord, Jesus Christ, and you will be saved ...*" What Paul refers to as the

"...*good works, which God prepared in advance for us to do.*" (Eph.2:10)

come after salvation – they can never earn it, or deserve it.

This leads us on to our second question: Why is it necessary? Why do I need this faith; this trust in Christ Jesus? And the simple answer is – in order to receive the same salvation that the Philippian jailer received. Not that my faith saves me! But I need faith in order to appropriate salvation for myself.

"*For it is by grace you have been saved, **through faith** – and this not from yourselves, it is the gift of God.*" (Eph.2:8 – emphasis added)

writes Paul to the Ephesians; while to the believers in Rome he writes:

"*...since we have been made right in God's sight* [i.e. been saved] ***by faith**, we have peace with God because of what Jesus Christ our Lord has done for us.*" (5:1 – emphasis added)

If I see a beggar in the street, with hand outstretched, I may be moved by compassion to go over and give him something. Now my gift is not, in any way, dependent on his outstretched hand; it is offered solely on the basis of my awareness of his pitiful state, and the love of my own heart. But he must have the outstretched hand in order to be able to accept my gift to him.

Father God looks on you and on me. He sees all of our self-righteousness as

"*filthy, menstrual-blood-soaked, rags*" (Is.64:6; cf. Zech.3:3ff).

But even 'though He sees us like that, God's love and grace and mercy are such that He offers us eternal life in Christ. Our faith is nothing more than the beggar's outstretched hand – but it is just as necessary. "Faith", someone has said, "is the only way by which men receive salvation."

In Heb.11:6 we are given a further reason for the necessity of faith, when the writer says that

"...*without faith it is impossible to please [God]*.",

and, indeed, this is perfectly logical! Because without faith, I do not trust; and if I do not trust Him, He is saddened.

Would you be saved? Then you must have this faith. Would you please God? Then you must have this faith.

A third reason why we must have this faith is that we can't see ahead of us! None of us knows, with certainty, what tomorrow will bring – never mind next week, or next year! But the attitude of the man of faith is "I don't know what the future holds; but I know Who holds the future"!

One of those named in the great gallery of faith in Heb.11, is Abraham.

> "*By faith, Abraham obeyed when he was called to go out to a place which he was to receive as an inheritance; and he went out, not knowing where he was to go.*" (v.8).

God's summons to him meant that Abraham had to leave home and family, and career and business; yet he went. He had to go out into the unknown; yet he went. Even in the best of us, there is a certain timorousness. We are almost afraid of what might happen to us if we take God at His word; if we act on His commands and promises.

A participant in the negotiations that led to the formation of the United Church of South India (1947) told how, in the protracted discussions, things were frequently held up by cautious and prudent people who wished to know just where each step was taking them, and what was likely to happen if they followed this course of action, or that. Eventually, the chairman had to remind them that a Christian – a disciple of Jesus – is one who has no right to ask where he is going!

It's true that most of us live a cautious life, on the principle of 'safety first'. But to live the life of the disciple of Jesus fully, necessitates a certain reckless willingness to adventure – and for that, we need an active, lively faith; a deep trust in God. It is a well-known maxim that, for the disciple of Jesus, faith is spelled with just four letters – R, I, S, K!

Prof Barclay has written: "If faith does not involve risk, it is not faith. If faith can see every step of the way, it is not faith. It is sometimes necessary for the Christian to take the right way, the way to which the voice of God is calling him, without knowing what the consequences will be. Like Abraham, he has to go out, not knowing where he is going."

We need faith in order that we may face the future with confidence – not in ourselves, or any human institution, but in the Sovereign God Who alone knows the end from the beginning; before Whom all of time and space are spread out.

And we need faith in order that our prayers be answered, our requests granted. James, in his letter, writes

> *"If any of you lacks wisdom, let him ask God, who gives to all men generously and without reproaching, and it will be given him. But let him ask in faith, with no doubting, for he who doubts is like a wave of the sea that is driven and*

tossed by the wind. For that person must not suppose that a double-minded man, unstable in all his ways, will receive anything from the Lord." (1:5-8).

And what James is saying is "Ask, and you shall receive – if you have faith!"

Mark records an episode in the earthly ministry of the Lord Jesus, just after the Transfiguration, when the disciples who had not been with Him on the mountain, were found to have been unable to bring healing to a demon-possessed boy. Jesus arrived, and asked them what was happening. He was told by the boy's father, who ended with these words:

> *"Have mercy on us and help us. Do something if you can." "What do you mean, `If I can'?" Jesus asked. "Anything is possible if a person believes." – if a person has faith!"* (9:22-23; *emphasis added*).

What is faith? – a complete and absolute trust in Almighty God, through the Lord, Jesus Christ.

Why is it necessary? – for many reasons: but certainly that I might be able to receive God's great offer of full salvation through that same Lord Jesus; that I might please Him; that I might face the future with confidence; and that my requests might be granted.

The final question we ask, then, must be, "How is it obtained?"

If faith is so important; if it is so necessary; if it effects so many areas of my life; how may I have it? Louis Berkhof, in his book '*Systematic Theology*', writes: "True saving faith ... [which] has its seat in the heart, and is rooted in the regenerate life ... is not, first of all, an activity of man [i.e. I can't produce it by myself], but a potentiality wrought by God in the heart of the sinner. ... It is only after God has implanted the seed of faith in the heart that men can exercise faith." (p.503).

So, the message from this theologian is that faith is, itself, a gracious gift from God. It isn't something that can be worked up, but something that comes down from above.

And, coming as a gift, it can only be accepted or rejected; coming as a gift, it may be asked for, but never demanded, or earned. So Paul, writing his great section on the gifts of God the Holy Spirit, in I Cor.12, can say that faith is one of those gifts and, in another place, can speak of faith being

"... built, not upon human wisdom, but upon the power of God." (I Cor.2:5).

Faith: clearly one of the most important concepts in the whole of the N.T. Everywhere it is required, and its importance insisted upon. It means abandoning all trust in one's own resources. It means casting oneself, unreservedly, on the mercy of God. It means laying hold of the promises of God, in Christ Jesus; relying entirely on His finished work for salvation – not on membership of a congregation, or any other organisation; not on good works; not on human parentage; but on Him – and on the power of God the Holy Spirit for daily strength to live our lives as He would have us live them. Faith implies complete reliance on God, and full obedience to God.

How important it is that we 'get to know it' – what it is; why it is necessary; how it is obtained. And not just an intellectual understanding of it, but a personal experience of it, that we might also receive God's gift of eternal life, here and now.

Chapter 2

REPENTANCE

"If you have sinned, do not lie down without repentance; for the want of repentance after one has sinned, makes the heart yet harder and harder."
(John Bunyan; 1628-1688)

In Luke's account of the Gospel, and at Chap.3, v.8, we read these words of John the Baptiser to those who came to hear him preach at the River Jordan:

> *"Prove by the way you live that you have repented of your sins and turned to God."*

And repentance is the word at which we look in this chapter. It's a word, I would suggest, that many folk would claim to be able to define but I want to ask three questions about the word in order to better understand it. Since many folk would, indeed, claim to be able to give an adequate definition, let's begin by asking that very question – "What does it mean?"

Right away, we must be aware that what it doesn't mean is 'Just being sorry'! So often, that sort of sorrow is only to do with the result, or consequence, of what we've done. So, if I rob a bank, and am caught, I will definitely be sorry – sorry for the consequences of my capture!

True repentance has to do with sorrow for what I've done – even if I appear to have "got away with it"! And it is shown in a turning from my own way to God's way. It involves a radical transformation of thought, attitude, outlook, and direction. J.B.Phillips, in his book *God, our Contemporary*, describes it as "... a fundamental change of outlook; the acceptance of a quite different scale of values." It is a turning from sin unto God and His service. It is a change of mind and heart. It's grief about, and hatred for, my sin. It's recognising that my sin is, first and foremost, against Almighty God Himself. So we read the words of the psalmist-king of Israel, David, addressed to the YHWH, after he had committed adultery with Bathsheba, and then arranged for the murder of her husband, Uriah the Hittite:

> "*Against You, You only, have I sinned and done what is evil from Your perspective; so that You are right in accusing me and justified in passing sentence.*" (Ps.51:4 [6]; Complete Jewish Bible).

Jesus told a parable about a farmer who had two sons. He called one of them and asked him to do some work in the field – and the son refused! So the father called the second son, and asked him to go – and he promised that he would.

But then, said Jesus, the situation changed. For the first son, having thought about his reaction, decided that he would, after all, go and work in the field. Meanwhile, the second son – who had promised that he would go and attend to the work – forgot his promise, and went off to do something else. Jesus asked the question:

> "*Which of the two obeyed his father?*" (Matt.21:31).

The answer, of course, is that it was the first one who, although he had said that he wouldn't do the work, changed his mind, and did it. He repented.

Perhaps one of the best-known of Jesus' parables is the one that we call the parable of the prodigal (wasteful) son. Once again, a father and two sons are involved. The younger son demands his inheritance from his father, and the father agrees to give it to him. The son then goes off to another country where he wastes his inheritance in high living. However, eventually and inevitably, his money ran out, and he ended up having to accept a job as a swineherd – surely the ultimate degradation for a Jewish boy! But it was as he was tending the pigs, and finding even the swill on which they were being fed to be appetising, that

"... *he came to himself* ..." (Luke 15:17)

– and that was when he decided to go back and throw himself on his father's mercy. He had a change of heart and mind; he took a different attitude to so much; he repented.

These two instances show, as does that third chapter of Luke's account of the Gospel narrative, that repentance has a very practical aspect. It's a change of mind and attitude; but it results in action – one son going to work; the prodigal returning home – and to a greater welcome than he would ever have thought to be possible; people sharing clothing and food; tax collectors taking no more than they should take; soldiers no longer extorting money, or making false accusations – and being content with their pay.

And John's initial words to the crowds were,

"*Prove by the way you live that you have repented of your sins and turned to God. Don't just say to each other, 'We're safe, for we are descendants of Abraham.' That means nothing, for I tell you, God can create children of Abraham from these very stones."* (Luke 3:8-9).

In other words, show your repentance; don't merely claim religious tradition, or ordinances.

"The crowds asked, 'What should we do?'" (3:10).

"What shall we **do**?"! They realised that action was necessary. 'Words', we are often told, 'are cheap'! Don't just say that you're sorry for what you have done, or said, or failed to do or say – show it!

This is true within the Jewish faith in which the Lord Jesus was raised. At Yom Kip'pur – the Jewish Day of Atonement (see ch.6) – there is, for the sincere Jew, a period of self-examination. Indeed, I suspect that when Paul encouraged disciples of Jesus, as they approached the Lord's table, to examine themselves (I Cor.11:28), he had that particular tradition in mind. One modern rabbi has written that

"In Judaism, repentance consists of two things: a change of heart and a change of action. True repentance requires our commitment and resolve, but it also has to manifest itself in action. Psalm 34:14 makes this clear: "Turn from evil and do good; seek peace and pursue it." Changing our life patterns is a twofold motion — turning from bad toward good. When we engage in these two actions, we are shaped for the better and honour God.

Repentance not only puts us on the right path — it brings us to a fuller understanding of the nature of God. It puts us in a posture of humility and reminds us that we worship a holy God Who demands our holiness. When we fall short of that standard, we must repent.

In that process of asking for forgiveness, we are reminded that our God is just and righteous. But in receiving His forgiveness, we are reminded that God is also merciful and loving. Ezekiel 33:11 assures us that God desires our repentance: "As surely as I live, declares the Sovereign Lord, I take no pleasure in the death of the wicked, but rather that they turn from their ways and live." And Psalm 103:13 tells us, "As a father has compassion on his children, so the Lord has compassion on those who fear Him."

Thus God not only offers us mercy, but eagerly desires that we take Him up on this amazing gift. When we keep both sides of God's nature in view — His justice and His mercy — we come to a more accurate understanding of who He is. *Yom Kip'pur* invites us to reflect on these ideas, see ourselves for the sinful people we are, and then to bridge that gap through the act of repentance." (Rabbi Yechiel Eckstein; *International Fellowship of Christians and Jews)*

The Latin translation of the word basically means "Growing wise again". It's a matter of getting ourselves back to what we should be. We've lost our way; we aren't what we should be; we don't do what we should do. And we need to change!

Repentance: a recognition that my sin is against God – regardless of who else has been affected by it; and a turning from my way to God's way, in a change of heart and attitude that leads to positive action.

But why is repentance necessary? The great prophet, Isaiah, spoke these familiar words:

"*All of us, like sheep, have strayed away. We have left God's paths to follow our own.*" (Isa 53:6).

The singer, Frank Sinatra, had a great hit with his song "I did it my way". Have you ever actually listened to the words of that song? It finishes like this:

"For what is man, what has he got?
If not himself, then he has naught
To say the things he truly feels and not the words of one who kneels.
The record shows I took the blows, and did it my way!
Yes, it was my way." (*emphasis added*)

And it's because we are all, by nature, going our own way – often blindly, often in panic, often heedless of the dangers that are ahead; that we need to repent, we need to change direction and go in the way which God has planned for us. We need to do it "His way"! We need to get our minds back to the way they were meant to be, in the plan of Almighty God. We need to reject sin – not primarily because it hurts other people, although it does; not even because it hurts us, although it does; but because it is an offence to God

But repentance is also one of the conditions of the Christian life, and of entry to the Kingdom of God. This necessity is clear in the Biblical record. Jesus began His public ministry with the message

> "*Repent, for the Kingdom of heaven is at hand.*" (Matt.3:2).

One of His final pronouncements, before His ascension, was

> "*... that repentance and forgiveness of sins should be preached in His Name to all nations, beginning from Jerusalem.*" (Luke 24:47).

And, of course, in the carrying out of that commission, no word is more significant than that of Peter on the following Day of Pentecost:

> "*Repent, and be baptized every one of you in the Name of Jesus Christ for the forgiveness of your sins; and you shall receive the gift of the Holy Spirit.*" (Acts 2:38).

To the same effect is Paul's declaration that, although God, in His mercy, had overlooked the ignorance of people with regard to their thinking about His Person, His command (not just polite suggestion!) now is for

> "... *everyone everywhere to repent of their sins and turn to Him.*" (Acts 17:30).

So we discover that, without repentance there is no salvation. But this doesn't interfere with the complimentary truth that we are saved through faith. The compilers of the New Bible Dictionary make plain that "Faith alone is the instrument of justification. But ..." they go on to say, "... justification is not the whole of salvation, and faith is not the only condition. ... Faith is directed to Christ for salvation from sin unto holiness and life. But this involves hatred of sin, and turning away from it. Repentance is turning from sin to God." (in loc). In other words, we might say that faith and repentance are two sides of one coin.

The words of the exalted Jesus, to the church in Laodicea,

> "*Behold I stand at the door and knock; if anyone hears my voice and opens the door, I will come in to him, and eat with him, and he with Me.*" (Rev.3:20),

are often used – erroneously, but understandably – as an invitation to repentance in evangelistic situations. They are, of course, spoken not to unbelievers, but to those who claim to be believers; disciples of Jesus; followers of the Christ. But regardless of who are the hearers of those words, we ought not to take them out of context. And the immediately preceding words are words, not of invitation, but of exhortation and command to

> "... *be zealous – and repent*"!

Repentance – necessary because we are like wayward sheep, and as a condition of salvation in Christ.

What does it mean? Why is it necessary? And the third question, which is of paramount importance, is how does it happen?

How does repentance come about? It's a question to which a variety of answers may be given. Often, repentance comes about through the preaching of God's Word. The message of the Book of Jonah, so often overshadowed by debate as to whether, or not, a man could actually have survived for three days in the stomach of any great fish, is a message of repentance. For we read that Jonah eventually went to Nineveh and proclaimed the Word of the Lord – taking nothing from it; adding no embellishments. And then we read that

> "... *the people of Nineveh believed God; they proclaimed a fast, and put on sackcloth, from the greatest of them to the least of them.*" (Jonah 3:5).

They repented; they changed from their sinful ways and attitudes; **because they had heard the Word of the Lord**.

And, praise God, the same thing still happens. Where the Word of God is faithfully proclaimed, just as it is, God works, and people repent and believe.

But, sometimes, repentance takes place because of a time of sorrow, or trouble. Many times, when I was in full-time pastoral ministry and regularly visiting folk in hospital, someone would remark, "You know, being here gives you a lot of time to think." And it is often as we thus think, that God the Holy Spirit convicts us of our sinfulness, and brings us to the place of repentance.

Repentance may also come about through joy, as a person becomes acutely aware of their utter unworthiness of all of God's goodness;

of the blessings that He pours out, even on the ungodly; and, in gratitude, repents of their sin, turning **to** God, in Christ.

For another, it may be the emptiness of the life that is being lived; the dawning realisation that there must be more to life than mere existence; and the discovery that Jesus came that we might have

"*... a rich and satisfying life.*" (John 10:10; NLT).

And this leads to a desire to have that life, and the realisation that repentance is necessary in order to have it.

Yet again, there are those who are drawn to the place of repentance because of the consistent Christian living of others. They see, in them, that this whole business of following Jesus – of being His disciple – isn't just a one-hour-a-week affair, but that it permeates their whole being; their every action. And they, too, learn that it begins with repentance.

Of course, we must never forget the place of a healthy fear of an eternity without Christ! But that will, if the repentance is genuine, be accompanied by one or other of the reasons already given.

However, nothing that I have said should be taken to mean that repentance is a one-off action! Every time I sin, I am required to repent. And since, as personal experience verifies, I am constantly falling into sin, then I need constantly to come to Father God to repent, and to seek, afresh, His forgiveness. And the wonder of His grace is such that, every time I do; every time I claim the atoning blood of the Son; every time, as the old preachers were wont to put it, that I stand under the cleansing flow; I receive that forgiveness – fully and freely!

Repentance.

What does it mean? A grief about, and hatred for, my sin that recognises that my sin is, primarily, against Father God Himself; that leads to a turning from my way to God's way; and that issues in an active demonstration of the change in my attitudes.

Why is it necessary? Because, in my fallen, sinful, nature I want to go my own way; because it is a necessary condition of salvation.

How does it happen? By the preaching of the Word; through sorrow, or joy; because of an awareness of an emptiness in life; by the consistency of others; – and all leading to a conviction of my sinfulness, and a realisation of my need. And it must be repeated, time and time again, until that Day when I see my Saviour in glory and, because it cannot even exist in His holy presence, am free from sin for eternity.

Have you repented? Are you truly sorry for your sins? Do you recognise that it is against God, Himself, that you have sinned; that it is His heart that you have broken? Do you want to experience God's forgiveness, and know His salvation? Then come to Him, in humility and truth; and in the assurance that He never turns away those who do approach Him, in Christ.

Chapter 3

CONVERSION

"Restore to me the joy of Your salvation, and uphold me by Your generous Spirit. Then I will teach transgressors Your ways, and sinners shall be converted to You."
(Psalm 51:12-13)

My current favourite version of the written Word of God is the New Living Translation. But, of course, I do make considerable use of many other versions, including the King James/Authorised Version

And there are times, I have to admit, when an older translation makes a particular point with what I believe to be a force that is missing in some of the more modern – albeit, often, more accurate – translations.

One such place is the 3rd verse of the 18th chapter of Matthew's account of the Gospel where, in the A.V., we read these words of the Lord Jesus:

> *"Verily I say unto you, except ye be converted, and become as little children, ye shall not enter into the Kingdom of God."*

"Except ye be converted ..."

'Conversion' is, sadly, another of those words that, at least in the Christian sense of the word, has been out of favour for some time. It's looked upon by many as an emotional word; not really suitable for late 20th/early 21st century adults. But here, we see it as a word that comes from the lips of the Lord Jesus, Himself and, as such, if we're at all serious about Him, it must demand our attention.

Of course, it is a word that is not unknown in everyday speech. If I go on holiday to another country, I will have to convert some of my British pounds to the currency of that country. And, of course, that is for me a change for the better. The converted currency may be spent in a way that the unconverted currency could not be!

I'm old enough to remember when the whole of the United Kingdom was given natural gas, from under the North Sea, in place of the manufactured gas that had been in use for many decades. However, differences in the two forms of gas meant that household appliances all had to be adapted in order to use the new form. And so, every gas-using household in the country had to be converted – a change that was for the better.

In looking at this word from a Biblical perspective, I want to look at the conversion experiences of three people as they're recorded for us in the book of the Acts of the Apostles. The relevant passages are Acts 9:1-20; and 16:11-40. The first account is of the Damascus Road experience of Saul of Tarsus – a deeply religious man; and the second covers both the story of Lydia – the successful business-woman in a man's world; and that of the Philippian gaoler – almost certainly a rough, coarse, uneducated fellow. But all three needed to be converted; they needed to experience God's great salvation; they needed to commence the process of sanctification. Each of them needed a personal encounter with Jesus.

As we consider these three people, we may note that the experience of conversion may differ.

You see, salvation is an intensely personal experience. And so, while the fact of conversion is the same for every true follower of Jesus, the form of it may be totally different. Consider the clarity with which Saul's conversion was marked

He would always be able to put an exact time to his conversion experience! It was indelibly printed on his heart and mind. He met with the Christ – and knew Him! Even as he asked the question *"Who are you ...?"* the realisation flooded his soul. And so, the question ended up as *"Who are You – Lord?"* This was Saul's encounter with Jesus – a dramatic experience such that it has become part of our everyday language, and even unbelievers speak of a "Damascus Road experience"! And this encounter made such a great impression on Saul that he would later be able to testify before king Agrippa, that it was

> *"At mid-day, O king, I saw, on the way, a light from heaven."* (26:13).

Not only the day, but also the very hour of his conversion, was clearly marked in Saul's memory, as the highly religious man, who had been persecuting those who were known as the 'Followers of the Way', surrendered to the Saviour of the world.

But if the conversion of Saul was marked by its clarity, that of Lydia was marked by its quietness.

> *"The Lord opened her heart, and she accepted what Paul was saying."* (16:14).

That was it! That was all that was necessary! There was no blinding light for Lydia; no conscious struggle. She was one who was, albeit unconsciously, seeking. She was, Dr. Luke records,

> *"a worshipper of God."* (Acts 16:14).

Oh, she had everything that the world could offer her – the same things that so many seek today: financial security; material possessions; social and professional status. But there was an emptiness in her heart that none of these things could fill; a longing that they could not satisfy. She knew well the truth of the relatively modern saying that "There's a God-shaped blank in every heart that only God can fill"; or, as Augustine had, much earlier, put it: "Our hearts are restless 'til they find their rest in Thee."

But, whether, or not, she could afterwards recall the exact moment, the important thing was that her heart was opened, and Jesus came in.

Saul was fighting Jesus; Lydia was seeking the peace that only He can bring. And then there was the gaoler! And we may note, concerning his conversion, its suddenness.

Here was a man who went to bed with absolutely no interest in the living God at all; but who, by the morning, was a disciple of Jesus! He may not have been interested in God – but God was most certainly interested in him!

A clear conversion for the man whose ideas about Jesus were not only wrong, but also positively antagonistic; a quiet conversion for the woman who was on the right road, and who merely needed to be led a little further along; a sudden conversion for the man who may never before have heard about Jesus and who, if he had, wouldn't have given a button for Him. How much the experience of conversion can differ from one individual to another. How gracious of Almighty God to deal with us on such an individual, and personal, basis. How important it is not to try to force ourselves into the mould of another's experience – or to insist that others have shared our own!

But let's move on to note that the essence of conversion is divine.

That is to say, the essential quality, or ingredient, of a true conversion experience is not human – it is from God. It's got nothing to do with an emotion that we may work up; but everything to do with the grace of God that pours down! And, as we look at our examples, we can see that the light of God's truth is revealed.

Here, we make specific reference to the conversion of Saul. Because not only did he see a physical light that blinded him; he also received spiritual light that illumined him. He saw where he'd been wrong; he saw that he'd been relying too much on "the traditions of the elders", and not enough on the Word of the Living God. Conversion, for him, involved a very real encounter – and had little to do with emotion. It was a turning around; a going in the opposite direction to that in which he had been travelling through life.

Now, he saw the truth of what he had previously heard. He learned, as have all who have trodden the same path, that commitment, and obedience, to Jesus doesn't involve a setting aside of learning and knowledge, but a gaining of it as one yields to Him

> "... in Whom are hid all the treasures of wisdom and knowledge." (Col.2:3).

And he realised the futility of all man-made 'gods' – whether they are made of wood, and metal, and stone; or are the 'gods' of ideology. In conversion, the light of God's truth is revealed, and the life of God's Son is received.

This was all that happened to Lydia. She just opened her heart and let Jesus in. I sometimes recall the words that I prayed on the evening of my own conversion experience – an experience not unlike Lydia's: "Come into my heart, Lord Jesus; come into my heart today. Come into my heart, Lord Jesus; forever with me to stay". He came – and He has stayed!

And He comes, not in order to impoverish; but to enlighten, enrich, enable. You just can't live the life of a disciple of Jesus without Him. As John put it in his first letter:

> "*He who has the Son, has life; he who has not the Son, has not life.*" (I John 5:12)!

And that's it! How much more clearly can God speak through His Word?! If you have received the Son, you are spiritually alive in Him; if you have not received the Son, you are spiritually dead in sin. And there's no other option! There's no 'third way'. According to the written Word of God, you are in – or you are out!

Is this, then, discrimination?! Of course not! Because every individual is welcome. Indeed, Father God

> "*... desires all men to be saved and to come to the knowledge of the truth.*" (I Tim 2:4).

Each one, consciously or unconsciously, makes his own decision!

In a true conversion experience, the light of God's truth is revealed; the life of God's Son is received; and the love of God's Spirit is released.

And this is the aspect that is most clearly seen in the story of the Philippian gaoler. When Paul and Silas were brought, bruised and bleeding, and placed in his charge, there was no physical assistance, no word of sympathy. But when he was converted, we read:

> "*... he took them, the same hour of the night, and washed their wounds.*" (Acts 16:33).

His conversion brought about a new attitude to others. With the new life that he received came a new love that he displayed – a love that, while it would be manifest to all men, was especially

"... *to those of the household of faith.*" (Gal.6:10).

Indeed, to talk of Christian love, without the new life in Christ, is futile – it just can't exist!

Light, life, love. And all of these are divine gifts. The Lord offers them – all that you and I have to do is to accept. But remember, that if we don't accept, then we have already rejected!

Finally, we may note that the effect of conversion is dynamic.

Conversion means a complete change of attitude; a new direction of travel. And not only a new direction of travel, but the only worthwhile direction – God's direction.

Of course there are those – some of whom might even wear a clerical collar! – who claim that it doesn't matter what a person believes as long as they are sincere. But this is nonsense. Indeed, the more sincere a person is, the more important it is that their beliefs are right! It's all too easy, and dangerous, to be sincerely wrong. Just ask the man who believes sincerely that he is driving the right way as he travels down the off-ramp from the motorway and suddenly meets all the oncoming traffic! There are countless instances of people who, under the influence of a mind-bending drug, have jumped out of upper-storey windows, sincerely believing that they could fly! Their lying in a heap on the ground below, just a few seconds later, was the proof that their belief was wrong – and often fatal.

So, the converted life will be marked by certain changes. There will be a change of purpose.

Consider Saul. He'd been doing pretty well in his own sphere. He had an important position; he had an impeccable pedigree; he was, academically, well qualified; he had abundant material possessions; he was well thought of by the Jewish authorities. But later, in referring to all of his earlier attainments, he terms them as garbage – indeed, the word he uses, *skubalon*, speaks of animal excrement; that which is worthless and detestable; the dregs. Once again, the AV translators probably got it right with the word "*dung*"! Now, however, most of his Pharisaic friends would have thought him mad – certainly that was the verdict of the Roman governor, Festus (Acts 26:24). To forsake all that he had, and was, in order to follow this Galilean Preacher Who, as far as they were concerned, was dead anyway!

But history has proved that Saul made the right choice. We would probably never have heard of Saul of Tarsus, if he hadn't become the apostle Paul – although making a name for himself would never have entered into his calculations – for he saw that the most important thing in life is to be a servant, a slave, of Jesus Christ.

But, coupled with a change of purpose, will be a change of pocket.

And here we look at Lydia. She must have been a fairly wealthy woman; "a seller of purple goods" usually was, for an expensive dye was used. But when she was converted, the Lord opened her home and her hands as well as her heart. She didn't lose any of her wealth – but she used it in a different way.

> "*When she and the members of her household were baptised,*"

records Dr Luke,

"she invited us to her home. 'If you consider me a believer in the Lord,' she said, "come and stay at my house." And she persuaded us." (v.15).

She was converted – and she immediately offered hospitality to the Lord's servants; she was involved in giving.

Not a week passes by without me receiving a number of appeals from *bona fide* Christian ministries appealing for financial support. But I believe that this shouldn't be necessary! And if those who claim to be members of the Body of Christ were all, as according to the Bible they should be, converted people, then there'd be such a change of pocket, that appeals wouldn't be necessary!

There is an interesting episode in the Old Testament that may be seen as being relevant. In Exodus 36 we read:

"The Lord has gifted Bezalel, Oholiab, and the other skilled craftsmen with wisdom and ability to perform any task involved in building the sanctuary. Let them construct and furnish the Tabernacle, just as the Lord has commanded. So Moses summoned Bezalel and Oholiab and all the others who were specially gifted by the Lord and were eager to get to work. Moses gave them the materials donated by the people of Israel as sacred offerings for the completion of the sanctuary. But the people continued to bring additional gifts each morning. Finally the craftsmen who were working on the sanctuary left their work. They went to Moses and reported, 'The people have given more than enough materials to complete the job the Lord has commanded us to do!' So Moses gave the command, and this message was sent throughout the camp: 'Men and women, don't prepare any more gifts for the sanctuary. We have enough!' So the people stopped bringing their sacred

offerings. Their contributions were more than enough to complete the whole project." (Ex.36:1-7).

What a difference it would make to the Lord's work today, if His people

"who are called by His Name"

were to contribute more than enough to complete the whole project – not of building a physical tabernacle, but of seeing the Gospel proclaimed to all nations!

A change of purpose; a change of pocket; and a change of person.

In v.29 of that 16th chap., we read that the gaoler was

"trembling with fear."

But just a few verses on, the record reads that

"He, and his entire household, rejoiced because they all believed in God." (v.34).

From fear, to joy – because he was converted!

You see, the life of the disciple of Jesus is exciting and exhilarating. It's not some boring routine of church attendance, prayer, and Bible reading – although many could do with a lot more of all of those! But there's a new dynamic; a new power; in life. There is the

"... fruit of the Spirit – love: joy, peace, patience, kindness, goodness, faithfulness, gentleness, self-control." (Gal.5:22-23),

the means by which life may <u>be</u> enjoyed! True disciples of Jesus are joyful people; and anyone who calls him/herself a Christian and doesn't have this deep, unquenchable, joy – regardless of situation or circumstances – is only a caricature of the real thing. The true believer is irrepressibly happy, because his joy isn't dependent on external conditions, but is the result of a cataclysmic change within.

Have you been converted? Are you changed? Have you turned from self to the Saviour? You may not be able to put a date on when it happened; on when you received new life in Christ; but that doesn't matter. The important thing is that you have it.

If I stand at the edge of the deep end of my local swimming pool and dive, or jump, in then the precise moment at which I enter the water may be easily determined. If I go to the seaside and walk bare-footed along the beach, perhaps in conversation with a companion, I may suddenly become aware that the water is lapping around my ankles – but I will have no idea of the precise moment at which I entered it! However, what is important is that I be found in the water – however I may have arrived at that state. It's the same with conversion. Some are able to pinpoint the precise moment and place; others are unable to do that, but are no less certain of their standing before God. They have "entered the water". And if you have – you'll know! Emotion does sometimes have a part to play – but it's not essential. All you have to do is to ask Him to take over, and start living your life for Him. It's the greatest, the only worthwhile, way to live. And conversion, according to Jesus, is an absolute necessity.

"*Except ye be converted ... ye shall not enter.*" (Matt.18:3).

Those aren't my words – they're His!

The experience may differ; but the essence is always divine; and the effect? – dynamite!

Chapter 4

SALVATION

*"There's a way back to God, from the dark paths of sin;
There's a door that is open, and you may go in.
At Calvary's cross is where you begin
When you come, as a sinner, to Jesus."*

In this chapter, the word at which we look is that great word 'salvation'. The New Testament writers use different Greek words to refer to salvation. Two of the most commonly used words are *charisma* and *dorea* – words that emphasize the gracious and absolutely free quality of the gift. Salvation cannot be earned, deserved, or purchased. It is a gracious gift of a gracious God.

In order to get to know this word better; to gain a deeper understanding of it; I want to do what I did with the word 'faith', and ask three questions about it – although they are different questions.

Salvation and its related words are, of course, also used in everyday conversation. We speak, especially in these cost-conscious days, of saving fuel, and food, and if we can, money. We speak of a person being saved from almost certain death. We even speak of someone having tried desperately, but having failed to save someone's life. We marvel at the way in which the skill of doctors and nurses, in combination with the wonders of modern medical and surgical knowledge and procedures, save many lives in emergency operations. We can be saved from dangerous situations; and even from those that would have been merely unpleasant. But when we turn to the written Word of God, the Bible and, particularly, to the N.T.; when we consider salvation as a word and concept of the Christian faith; what is it, then, that we are saved from?

In Acts 2:40, after Peter's great sermon on that first Day of Pentecost of the Christian era; that 'birth-day' of the Christian Church; we read that

> "... he testified with many other words and exhorted them, saying 'Save yourselves from this crooked generation.'"

That is to say, there is, in spite of what evangelical preachers – myself included – preach about salvation being all of God's grace, there is a sense on which we do have a part to play. It's to do with our response, and how we live out the Christian life-style into which we have entered. I must be careful where I go; what I do; with whom I spend my time. I must do all that I can to keep myself from being tainted by the world's values – a life revolving around Big Brother, or East Enders, or Britain's got Talent; infected by its greed, and selfishness, and lust. The person who has experienced the salvation of Christ should have a sort of antiseptic quality about him/her that enables them to walk in the world, yet be able to keep themselves free from the ungodly influence of the world.

As Paul makes clear, in his letter to the believers in Ephesus, I must

> "*Put on the whole armour of God.*" (6:11).

It is not sufficient that the armour is provided – I must appropriate it for myself! These are the conditions that are attached.

But I am also saved from 'lostness'. Luke records a saying of Jesus that

"... *the Son of Man came to seek and to save the lost.*" (19:10).

How many people there are in the world, today, who are lost! They just don't know which way to turn – and many will not be slow in telling you! And so, all too often, they turn the wrong way – to alcohol, or some other drug; to infidelity, or abusive behaviour; to vandalism or violence.

The message of the Christian Gospel is that Jesus came to rescue such people – to save them; that He came to turn men and women from the ways that lead only to eternal death – to the Way that leads to eternal life, even Himself. A letter that I received from the Christian radio broadcaster FEBA (The Far East Broadcasting Association), as I was working on this chapter, contained this amazing statement: "The human heart is designed for Jesus ... but the lost just don't know it yet."! What a wonderful call to mission.

Saved from godless influences; saved from lostness; and saved from sin. This is probably the way in which we usually think of salvation within a Christian context. But what, then, is sin?! "Sin is any transgression of, or want of conformity to, the law of God." is how the Westminster divines defined it in the Shorter Catechism. And the Bible speaks of sin in different ways, each of which tells us a little more about it:

The most common New Testament word for 'sin' (*hamartia*) speaks of a 'falling short'; 'missing the mark'; 'going off the straight'; or 'going too far'. It's a word that comes from the world of sport, and we might illustrate it in two ways. In archery, the sport in which it was first used, there is a bull's-eye for which the archer aims. Now, if my arrow hits the bull, or the mark, I gain the prize; but, if it misses the mark, whether by only a fraction of an inch, or by a couple of feet, then I don't get anything! And if it falls short of the target, or overshoots it, whether by six inches, or six yards, I am still not awarded the prize.

The other sport/game at which we might look is the game of skittles – what is basically being played in a modern bowling alley. In that game, the objective is to knock down all of the skittles with one bowl of the ball – and this requires a good straight bowl. But if the ball goes off the straight, by however little; or if it isn't bowled hard enough and fails to even reach the skittles; then I have failed in my objective.

Sin is failing to keep God's law perfectly. Some, it is true, keep it better than others – but no-one 'hits the mark'; no-one 'knocks down all of the skittles'; no-one manages, always, to keep to the 'straight and narrow'. So Paul is able to state, quite categorically, that

> "*All have sinned, and fallen short of God's glory.*" (Rom.3:23).

But this could, and often is, an almost unconscious sinning. And so we find that God, knowing the human heart as He alone does, uses another word – *parabasis* – usually translated as 'transgression'.

This speaks of a deliberate stepping over the boundary; or of going 'out of bounds' either by carelessness, or neglect. It is with transgression that the idea of guilt appears, because we know that what we are doing, or failing to do, is wrong in God's eyes. There is nothing accidental, or unconscious about transgression, making it a more serious word and concept than missing the mark!

Then there is 'iniquity' (Hebrew – *ayan*; Greek – *adikia*). This is the word that is most common in the O.T., although it is also found frequently enough in the New. There are, in fact, a number of words, with slightly different shades of meaning. However, the common denominator is that iniquity signifies a distortion, or perversion, that is at the very heart of the personality. It has to do with attitude as much as action/inaction. It has been defined as "... being able to look into the face of God, with eyes that seem to denote concentration and devotion, whilst all of the time our hearts are already set on going after that which displeases, and dishonours Him." (possibly Rev George B. Duncan!). But God sees, and knows, even our hearts.

The fourth term is what we call 'rebellion'. This is a Hebrew concept (*merah*), and refers, basically, to a deliberate refusal to do the will of God. In every heart, it has been said, is a cross and a throne. Rebellion is putting self on the throne, and leaving only a cross for the Lord.

Finally, there is 'wickedness' (Hebrew – *ra*; Greek – *ponria*). This is the end result of this steady progression in sin; it is the state in which a man is left as a result of sin in all of its other forms. Read Rom.1:18ff for Paul's catalogue of wickedness – and then thank God that the salvation of which the Christian Gospel speaks, is a salvation from sin – its power; its penalty; and, eventually, even its presence.

Saved from evil influences; saved from lostness; saved from sin; and saved from wrath. In our fallen, human nature, you and I deserve only the wrath and terrible judgement of Almighty God. Because we are sinful mortals, and He is the pure and sinless One, we deserve only to be banished from His presence into everlasting darkness. But the offer made in the scriptures is of salvation from even that; of a new relationship with God, through which I will be saved from His wrath – a relationship, not of Creator and created, but of Father and child.

What a salvation this is! How many things – and how powerful and frightening they are – that I am saved from! But if I am to be saved from all of that, then I need to know how. I need to know by what, or by Whom, or in what manner I am saved.

How is it that there can be such a wonderful salvation? And the simple answer is "Through the death of Christ".

> "*God loved the world so much that He gave His only-begotten Son; that everyone who believes in Him, should not perish, but have eternal life.*" (John 3:16).

God loved, and loves, you and me so much that, in the Persona of the Lord Jesus – God the Son – He gave Himself that we might know His salvation. It is the Father Who, in love, planned this salvation; it is the Son Who, in obedience, provides this salvation; and it is Holy Spirit Who, by His indwelling power, personalises this salvation – making it real to all who do believe, and put their trust in the Christ.

Salvation, then, is based on love. It is not something that I deserve; it is not something that I can earn; it is God's gracious gift. And it is a full salvation. Once I obtain it, I need nothing else. In accepting God's offer of it, I am reconciled, forgiven, and cleansed; I pass from death into life; I receive the assurance that I am now a child of God – a joint-heir with the Lord Jesus, possessing a life that is eternal in its quality, and everlasting in its duration, and that shatters the bondage of the fear of death.

And all of this is made possible because Jesus Christ hung on a cross; taking my place there – and yours; paying the penalty for my sin – and yours; showing the perfect obedience that neither you nor I is capable of showing; gaining my acquittal – and yours – by bearing our punishment.

"Bearing shame and scoffing rude,
in **my** place condemned **He** stood;
Sealed **my** pardon with **His** blood;
Hallelujah! What a Saviour." (Philip P. Bliss; *emphases added*)

What a Saviour, indeed! And it is by His death on the cross that I am saved.

Saved from; saved by; and saved for.

We've discovered why we need to be saved – all that we need to be saved from; we've remembered how it is that we may be saved – the means of that salvation; and so, finally, we look at the outcome of salvation. If I acknowledge my need; if I accept the offer; what happens next? What's it all for?

Peter, writing to a company of people who had experienced this salvation for themselves; a group who had 'been saved'; tells them

"... *you are a chosen race, a royal priesthood, a holy nation, God's own people, that you may declare the wonderful deeds of Him Who called you out of darkness into His marvellous light.*" (I Pet.2:9).

There is sufficient material there for a series of teaching messages, but those words certainly tell us that we are saved for two specific purposes. First of all, we are saved for holy living.

Now, some folk are put off by the word 'holy'. It speaks to them of something ultra-spiritual, and in the worst sense! It has come to mean, even to many who know little or nothing of the works of Rabbie Burns, to denote the person who is like Holy Willie – the sanctimonious hypocrite who is the subject of "Holy Willie's Prayer". But the word actually means 'consecrated', or 'different'. If I am saved, then I should be different from those who are not yet saved.

I confess to getting a little annoyed with those who seem to suggest that disciples of Jesus should be just like everyone else. For that is not what God tells us through His word. A Christian – a true disciple of Jesus; one who is not merely bearing the label – has a different outlook on life; different interests and pursuits; different priorities; a different attitude towards God; a different attitude towards sin; a different attitude towards the worship services; a different attitude towards prayer and Bible study. Things that formerly seemed to be a waste of time take on a new importance. And all of this is holy living. Christians are called, by God, to be different: to be lights in a world darkened by sin; to be seasoning for a tasteless humanity; to be a living fellowship of His own people.

Although I endeavour to always be true to the written Word of God, I don't believe that I am called to be what used to be termed a "Bible-thumper" – someone who harangues his listeners, almost beating them into some form of outward submission with much thumping of the pulpit Bible in an attempt to add emphasis to the spoken word. And, although I may make an occasional jocular comment while preaching, I don't believe that I am called to be a pulpit/platform entertainer. I don't know if Charles Haddon Spurgeon (1834-1892) preached like that. However, he did give the following admonition to the Church in the late 1800s – and his words apply just as much to the Church today as they did then – if not even more so!

"Feeding Sheep ... or Amusing Goats?

An evil is in the professed camp of the Lord, so gross in its impudence, that the most short-sighted can hardly fail to notice it during the past few years. It has developed at an abnormal rate, even for evil. It has worked like leaven until the whole lump ferments. The devil has seldom done a cleverer thing than hinting to the church that part of their mission is to provide entertainment for the people, with a view to winning them.

From speaking out as the Puritans did, the church has gradually toned down her testimony, then winked at and excused the frivolities of the day. Then she tolerated them in her borders. Now she has adopted them under the plea of reaching the masses.

My first contention is that providing amusement for the people is nowhere spoken of in the Scriptures as a function of the church. If it is a Christian work, why did not Christ speak of it? "Go ye into all the world and preach the gospel to every creature" (Mark 16:15). That is clear enough. So it would have been if He had added, "and provide amusement for those who do not relish the gospel." No such words, however, are to be found. It did not seem to occur to Him.

Then again, "He gave some, apostles; and some, prophets; and some evangelists; and some pastors and teachers ..., for the work of the ministry" (Eph.4:11-12). Where do entertainers come in? The Holy Spirit is silent concerning them. Were the prophets persecuted because they amused the people or because they refused? The concert has no martyr roll.

Again, providing amusement is in direct antagonism to the teaching and life of Christ and all His apostles. What was the attitude of the church to the world? "Ye are the salt" (Matt.5:13), not the sugar candy; something the world will spit out, not swallow. Short and sharp was the utterance, "Let the dead bury their dead" (Matt.8:22) He was in awful earnestness.

Had Christ introduced more of the bright and pleasant elements into His mission, He would have been more popular when they went back, because of the searching nature of His teaching. I do not hear Him say, "Run after these people Peter and tell them we will have a different style of service tomorrow, something short and attractive with little preaching. We will have a pleasant evening for the people. Tell them they will be sure to enjoy it. Be quick Peter, we must get the people somehow." Jesus pitied sinners, sighed and wept over them, but never sought to amuse them.

In vain will the Epistles be searched to find any trace of this gospel of amusement! Their message is, "Come out, keep out, keep clean out!" Anything approaching fooling is conspicuous by its absence. They had boundless confidence in the gospel and employed no other weapon.

After Peter and John were locked up for preaching, the church had a prayer meeting but they did not pray, "Lord, grant unto Thy servants that by a wise and discriminating use of innocent recreation we may show these people how happy we are." If they ceased not from preaching Christ, they had not time for arranging entertainments. Scattered by persecution, they went everywhere preaching the gospel. They turned the world upside down (Acts 17:6). That is the only difference! Lord, clear the church of all the rot and rubbish the devil has imposed on her, and bring us back to apostolic methods.

Lastly, the mission of amusement fails to effect the end desired. It works havoc among young converts. Let the careless and scoffers, who thank God because the church met them halfway, speak and testify. Let the heavy laden who found peace through the concert not keep silent! Let the drunkard to whom the dramatic entertainment has been God's link in the chain of the conversion, stand up! There are none to answer. The mission of amusement produces no converts. The need of the hour for today's ministry is believing scholarship joined with earnest spirituality, the one springing from the other as fruit from the root. **The need is biblical doctrine, so understood and felt, that it sets men on fire**." *(emphasis added).*

The problem is not that Christians enjoy themselves (who wants to belong to a boring, dry, dull church?), but that, too often, amusement is offered **at the expense of** preaching the Gospel and telling people the truth. Exhortation has been replaced by entertainment. I have long been concerned at the adulation given to certain ministries – both preachers and worship leaders. I have watched as some have performed – rather than provide

"*the whole counsel of God*" (Acts 20:27).

I think of the words of Paul:

"... the time is coming when people will not endure sound teaching, but having itching ears they will accumulate for themselves teachers to suit their own likings, and will turn away from listening to the truth and wander into myths." (II Tim.4:3-4).

Max Lucado writes; "When God-hungry souls walk into a congregation of wannabe superstars, what happens? When God seekers see singers strut like Las Vegas entertainers . . . When they hear the preacher – a man of slick words, dress, and hair – play to the crowd and exclude God . . . When other attendees dress to be seen and make much to-do over their gifts and offerings . . . When people enter a church to see God yet can't see God because of the church, don't think for a second that God doesn't react. "Be especially careful when you are trying to be good so that you don't make a performance out of it. It might be good theatre, but the God Who made you won't be applauding" (Matt.6:1; The Message)" (*Outlive Your Life: You Were Made to Make a Difference*).

We are saved, in order that we may declare the message of salvation. "Preach the Gospel at all times" said Francis of Assisi (allegedly!), "and, when necessary, use words." Others should see enough of Christ in my life and living to be attracted to Him. My words then become answers and explanations.

> *"Always be prepared to make a defence to anyone who calls you to account for the hope that is in you ..."* (I Peter 3:15).

We are to live lives that are seen to be different; and we are to tell others what the difference is! We are to share the Good News! I recall an old T.V. advert for a particular brand of beer in which, when the barman is asked for a pint, he remarks: "You've heard the good news, then?" On his receipt of an affirmative reply, one of the other drinkers says, "Well, pass it on, then!" If we have been saved; if we have truly experienced this great offer of salvation made to us by Almighty God; if we have appropriated it for ourselves; then we are the recipients of the best news that mankind can ever receive – and we are to pass it on!

Salvation – another of the great words of the Christian faith. Let us remember what it is we are saved from; what it is we are saved by; what it is we are saved for. But, most of all, let us be sure that we are saved; that we have accepted that wonderful offer of salvation. For, if we reject, or even neglect, it then we are assured, in the Letter to the early Hebrew believers, that there is no escape. (Heb.2:3)

Salvation – it's good to have some knowledge of what it means; it's far, far better to experience it in your own life.

Chapter 5

PROPITIATION/EXPIATION

"Herein is love, not that we loved God, but that He loved us, and sent His Son to be the propitiation for our sins."

(1 John 4:10; KJV)

In this chapter, we are going to look at what some might consider to be one of the more confusing of the great words of the Christian faith. That word is the word propitiation. The confusion is in the different ways in which the Greek word, *hilasterion*, is translated into the various English language translations of the Bible. The word is the Greek rendering of the Hebrew *kapporeth* which refers to the Mercy Seat of the Ark of the Covenant, and may be translated as either "propitiation" or "expiation" each of which refers to a different function of the Mercy Seat. Propitiation literally means *to make favourable* and specifically includes the idea of dealing with God's wrath against sinners. Expiation literally means *to make amends* and implies either the removal or cleansing of sin.

A major proponent of expiation was the theologian C.H.Dodd (1884-1973). He rejected the use of propitiation because he believed that it portrayed Almighty God as some kind of angry, vindictive Being Whose wrath could be averted by the satisfactory offering of the sinner – or his representative. Now, it is true that the God and Father of the Lord Jesus Christ is not that angry divinity requiring appeasement. But it is also true that 'propitiation' can also convey the more positive concept of a favourable disposition that is brought about by the removal of the cause of displeasure by the very One Who is offended, and at His cost.

So Leon Morris (1914-2006), the 'champion' of the use of 'propitiation' writes: "...the God of the Bible is not a Being who can be propitiated after the fashion of a pagan deity. ... the Bible writers have nothing to do with pagan conceptions of a capricious and vindictive deity, inflicting arbitrary punishments on offending worshippers, who must then bribe Him back to a good mood by the appropriate offerings." (*The Apostolic Preaching of the Cross*, p. 129).

We might sum it up – although to do so in a sentence or two is not doing the subject anything like full justice – by saying that expiation has the sense of a sacrifice that satisfies God's legal requirements, while propitiation has the sense of a sacrifice that satisfies the requirements of God's character. Expiation refers to that which is judicial; propitiation refers to that which is relational. Expiation removes a barrier; propitiation removes the barrier, **and** restores a relationship.

In one of his published works, William Barclay writes that "The supreme problem of life is, 'How can a man get into a right relationship with God? How can a man feel at peace, at ease, at home, with God? How can a man escape the feeling of estrangement and fear in the presence of God?'" Judaism answered these questions by saying that "A man can attain to a right relationship with God by a meticulous keeping of the law; a fulfilling of all of its works." But that was simply to say that it is impossible! And it is so, simply because man is, whatever the modern humanist and relativist may proclaim, a sinful, fallen, imperfect, creature who can never perfectly keep God's Law.

"Not the labours of my hands
Can fulfil Thy Law's demands" cries the hymn-writer.

All that the Law can do is to make me aware of my sin. Ignorance is, indeed, bliss! It is only when I know what I ought to be doing that I realise that I am not doing it! "It is only when a man knows the law and tries to satisfy it, that he realises he can never satisfy it" writes one commentator on Paul's Letter to the Romans. The law shows me my own weakness and sinfulness.

But does all of this mean that the way is cut off from God; that I may never attain a right relationship with Him? Praise His Name, it doesn't! Because the way to God is not the way of the Law, but the way of grace; it isn't the way of works, it's the way of faith. This is what Paul is saying in his letter to the Roman disciples of Jesus, in ch.3:23-28 (A.V.). And, in doing so, he uses three metaphors, bound up in just three words. He uses the metaphor of the law courts, using the term 'justification'; he uses the metaphor of slavery, using the term 'redemption'; and he uses the metaphor of sacrifice, using the term 'propitiation'. Redemption, and justification, we will look at later (chs. 9 & 11); but in this chapter, we are looking at that third word – propitiation. And we begin by thinking about the need for propitiation.

'Why is it necessary?' is the question that we ask here. And, in order to answer it, we must be sure of the basic meaning of, and background to, the word.

It's a word which, as we noted above, has to do with sacrifice. If it is indeed true, as Prof. Barclay put it, that the supreme problem of life is a broken relationship with God; it is also true that the supreme problem of a religion that is aimed at fellowship with God, is sin; for it is sin that interrupts that fellowship. And so, in every culture, man offered sacrifice to appease God; to, as it were, buy forgiveness for his sin.

The Jews, of course, were given their sacrificial laws directly by God, through Moses. And so, every evening, and every morning, the sin-offering was made. This was not for any particular sin committed by any individual, but for the nation as a whole – and that offering was made, twice every day, until the destruction of the Temple in Jerusalem.

C.H.Dodd uses the analogy of "... a powerful disinfectant ..." that removes the taint of sin; while another commentator speaks of sin as being "neutralised".

So we may say that propitiation is a means of dealing with sin, and that it is necessary because, as Paul reminds us

> "... all have sinned and fallen short of God's glory." (Rom.3:23).

It is necessary in order that the relationship that has been broken by sin, might be restored.

But we must go on to think about the means by which propitiation is accomplished or, to put it in the form of a question, the 'How?' of propitiation.

From what we have already learned, we might think that what is required is the re-establishment of a sacrificial system; that we should start to bring our lambs, and doves; our goats and bullocks; along to the church building for the minister/pastor to slay them as a means of making us right with God!

The problem with that, however, would be exactly the same as it has always been. As a human being with a fallen nature, I would leave the building, and sin again! Paul encapsulates the experience of each one of us when he writes to the early church in Rome:

> *"I have discovered this principle of life—that when I want to do what is right, I inevitably do what is wrong. I love God's law with all my heart. But there is another power within me that is at war with my mind. This power makes me a slave to the sin that is still within me. Oh, what a miserable person I am! Who will free me from this life that is dominated by sin and death?"* (7:21-24; NLT).

So, under that system of sacrifice for my sin, I would have to return, again and again, seeking that reconciliation with Almighty God.

But, of course, under the New Dispensation, the New Covenant, this is not the case. Paul continues, in Romans 3:

> *"Thank God! The answer is in Jesus Christ our Lord."* (v. 25)

In the Letter to the Hebrew disciples of Jesus, the writer reminds us that

> *"The sacrifices under that system were repeated again and again, year after year, but they were never able to provide perfect cleansing for those who came to worship. If they could have provided perfect cleansing, the sacrifices would have stopped, for the worshipers would have been purified once for all time, and their feelings of guilt would have disappeared.*
>
> *But instead, those sacrifices actually reminded them of their sins year after year. For it is not possible for the blood of bulls and goats to take away sins."* (Heb.10:1-4).

It was the whole of human experience that an animal sacrifice failed to make full propitiation; that, at best, it restored the relationship for a time – until sin again broke it. What was needed was a lasting sacrifice. And this, praise God, He Himself has provided! For, writes Paul,

> "God ... appointed [Jesus] as the means of propitiation, a propitiation accomplished by the shedding of His blood." (Rom.3:25; Phillips).

So the means by which propitiation is accomplished is the shed blood of Jesus.

> "... He has appeared once and for all to abolish sin by the sacrifice of Himself."

is how the writer to the Hebrews puts it. (9:26; Phillips).

Ray Boltz, one of the modern Christian-song-writers, sings a song entitled "One drop of blood". The chorus goes like this:

"One drop of blood fell to the scales;
It covered my transgressions and all the times I failed.
The enemy was mighty; he came in like a flood.
He was defeated by one drop of blood."

But all of this is no merely mechanical action, as Paul makes clear when he goes on, concerning Christ's sacrifice, that it is

> "... to be received and made effective in ourselves by faith." (Rom.3:26; Phillips).

You see, it's so easy to be deceived into thinking that the ritual is all that matters; that as long so Jesus died, all is well; that so long as we have some water sprinkled on us as infants, or are plunged under the water in believers' baptism all is well; that so long as we take some bread and some wine once in a while, all is well. But this just isn't so! Listen to some rather harsh-sounding words spoken by God through His prophet Isaiah:

> "*Listen to YHWH, you leaders of "Sodom."*
> *Listen to the law of our God, people of "Gomorrah."*
> *'What makes you think I want all your sacrifices?'*
> *says YHWH.*
> *'I am sick of your burnt offerings of rams*
> *and the fat of fattened cattle.*
> *I get no pleasure from the blood*
> *of bulls and lambs and goats.*
> *When you come to worship me,*
> *who asked you to parade through my courts with all your ceremony?*
> *Stop bringing me your meaningless gifts;*
> *the incense of your offerings disgusts me!*
> *As for your celebrations of the new moon and the Sabbath*
> *and your special days for fasting—*
> *they are all sinful and false.*
> *I want no more of your pious meetings.*
> *I hate your new moon celebrations and your annual festivals.*
> *They are a burden to me. I cannot stand them!*
> *When you lift up your hands in prayer, I will not look.*
> *Though you offer many prayers, I will not listen,*
> *for your hands are covered with the blood of innocent victims.*
> *Wash yourselves and be clean!*
> *Get your sins out of my sight.*
> *Give up your evil ways.*
> *Learn to do good.*
> *Seek justice.*
> *Help the oppressed.*

> *Defend the cause of orphans.*
> *Fight for the rights of widows.'"* (1:10-17; NLT)

And the same is true today. We must have a living and active faith and trust in the Lord Jesus, before His sacrifice has any meaningful effect. His sacrificial death must

> *"... be received by faith."* (Rom.3:25).

It isn't enough to go through the outward motions; there must be a corresponding cleansing deep within. Too many, I fear, like those to whom Isaiah first spoke, remain

> *"... lovers of self, lovers of money, proud, arrogant, abusive, disobedient to their parents, ungrateful, unholy, inhuman, implacable, slanderers, profligates, fierce, haters of good, treacherous, reckless, swollen with conceit, lovers of pleasure rather than lovers of God, holding the form of religion but denying the power of it."* (II Tim 3:2-5).

And Paul's advice – indeed, his exhortation?

> *"Avoid such people!"* (v.5).

The means by which propitiation is accomplished – the once-for-all sacrifice of Jesus Christ Himself, appropriated by each one of us as individuals.

Propitiation: the need for it; the means by which it is accomplished; and the result of it.

If I do appropriate this sacrifice of Jesus; His blood, shed on the cross; for myself, what happens? Well, obviously, the relationship between myself and God is restored. I am no longer just His creature, but truly His child – able to say "Abba, Father". I am, as Paul writes, in Romans 3, justified because of my faith in, and commitment to, Jesus. And, as we have already learned, that means – quite simply, and truly wonderfully – that Almighty God, the sinless One Who inhabits dimensions that are beyond our human comprehension, treats me "just-as-if-I'd"-never sinned!

Prof. Barclay writes: "The great basic truth behind this word is that it is through Jesus Christ that man's fellowship with God is first restored, then manifested ...... Through what He did, the penalty is remitted; the guilt is removed; the defilement is taken away."

The need for propitiation: that the relationship with God which is broken by my sin, might be restored; and the fact that

> "... *all have sinned and fallen short of God's glory.*"

Are you aware of; have you admitted; your need?

The means by which propitiation is accomplished: the shed blood of Jesus Christ – the once-for-all fully-atoning, sacrifice; and faith that appropriates that sacrifice for the individual. And it is that sacrifice that we remember every time we gather around His table. Have you exercised faith in appropriating it for yourself – or is all of this merely ritual:

> "... *holding the form of religion but denying the power of it.*" (II Tim.3:5)?

The result of propitiation: a restored relationship that sin can never again break; acceptance by Almighty God as a child of His grace; a life lived to His eternal glory.

Is that the sort of life that you and I are living? If we call ourselves disciples of Jesus; if we claim to be members of His body; if we come to His Table and identify ourselves there, as His; then it certainly ought to be – to the everlasting praise of His most holy Name.

Chapter 6

ATONEMENT

"... on this day atonement will be made for you, to cleanse you. Then, before YHWH, you will be clean from all your sins." (Lev.16:30; NIV)

Apart from a single instance in the Authorised Version (Rom.5:11), the word 'atonement' is found only in the Old Testament. It is not, however, either a strict translation, or even a transliteration (where the letters of the original are changed to Roman letters to form a word that may be read by those with no knowledge of the original language: the word 'baptism', from the Greek *'baptismo'*, is a case in point!) of either the Hebrew or Greek words that are found in the originals. In the case of 'atonement' the word was coined in order to make clear the meaning behind it – that of making 'at one' those who have been at variance with one another. It is indeed, closely linked to the word 'propitiation' at which we looked in the previous chapter.

In Rom.5:11 (A.V.), Paul refers to the Lord Jesus as the one

"... by whom we have now received the atonement."

In other words, he is making the astounding claim that it is in Jesus that God and man are made to be 'at one'! Using different terminology, he writes to the Corinthian church and says that God

"... *through Christ reconciled us to Himself and gave us the ministry of reconciliation; that is, in Christ God was reconciling the world to Himself, not counting their trespasses against them, and entrusting to us the message of reconciliation.*" (II Cor.5:18-19).

The reason why we need to be made 'at one' – to be reconciled – is, of course because of a relationship that has been broken! At the beginning of created time, we learn from the opening chapters of the book of Genesis – the book of 'Beginnings' – that God had a special relationship with the pinnacle of His creation, the only part of His creation of which He had said

"*Let Us make man in Our image, according to Our likeness*" (Gen. 1:26; NKJV).

We read that He provided a companion for the man,

"*an help meet for him*" (Gen.2:20; A.V.),

or 'a companion suitable for him'. And, from the 3rd chapter of Genesis (remembering that the chapter and verse divisions are not a part of any of the original texts, but were – at least as far as the ones with which we are familiar are concerned – a 16th century innovation designed to make it easier for people to find a particular passage when they wanted to do so; or when the preacher wanted them to do so!) we learn that Almighty God actually walked about in the garden in which He had placed the man and the woman. He talked with them, and they with Him. Can you even begin to imagine what that must have been like? To have enjoyed that kind of relationship with the Creator of all that is! A relationship, one would think, that was worth keeping, and guarding, and cherishing.

But, sadly, this highly desirable state of affairs did not continue. Most of us know the story well. We read, in Gen.3 that the creature, named as the serpent in English language translations, approached the woman, and asked her that insidious question:

"Did God say ... ...?"

The very character of Almighty God was being questioned. "Can you trust God? Don't you realise that He has an ulterior motive? Aren't you aware that He is just afraid that you will eat of the fruit, and become like Him, knowing good and evil? Why, all that stuff about 'dying' is just wool to pull over your eyes!" And the woman ate; and then the man ate; and the relationship was broken. They had disobeyed – and sin had been given entry to the human race. They had disobeyed – and all of creation was to be affected by their sin (see Gen.3:17).

But, praise God, He was not content to just let the man and the woman suffer the eternal consequences of their sin. And so, even before pronouncing His righteous judgement on the man and the woman, He made it clear that He desired the recovery of that relationship. And, right there, in Gen.3:15, in what theologians and scholars refer to as the *Protoevangelium* (the 'first Gospel'), He declares that the seed of the woman (and note, it is just the woman who is mentioned) shall bruise the head of the serpent – but not without personal cost. What a picture of Calvary – when the devil was defeated, but at the cost of the very life-blood of the Christ: He Who was born of woman, without any input by a man.

And then we have the first recorded sacrifice in the whole Bible as man's feeble attempt to cover up his own sinfulness, by his own works – the sewing together of aprons of fig leaves – is seen to be so inadequate. Only the shedding of blood could deal with sin (Heb.9:22) – and so Almighty God made the sacrifice that provided the covering that He would find to be, at least temporarily, acceptable:

> *"And YHWH Elohim made for Adam and for his wife garments of skins, and clothed them."* (Gen.3:21).

Already, the grace of God is being manifest on behalf of His fallen creation.

Throughout the Old Testament, we see this ritual of animal sacrifice continued. The book of Leviticus provides all of the rules and regulations that were to be observed as history marched, inexorably, on to the final, once-for-all, sacrifice of the perfect Lamb of God. But it was in that unique sacrifice that restoration was accomplished. It was in the death of Jesus of Nazareth, the Christ, that atonement was fully realised. It was as He gave Himself, willingly, in fulfilment of the Old Testament prophecies, that reconciliation was made.

It was the prophet Isaiah who had stated, of the coming Messiah,

> "*I gave my back to the smiters, and my cheeks to those who pulled out the beard; I hid not my face from shame and spitting.*" (50:6)

and who had been permitted, as it were, to peek into the mist of future time to see that the Suffering Servant

> "*... was despised and rejected by men; a Man of sorrows, and acquainted with grief; and as One from Whom men hide their faces He was despised, and we esteemed Him not.*
>
> "*Surely He has borne our griefs and carried our sorrows; yet we esteemed Him stricken, smitten by God, and afflicted. But He was wounded for our transgressions, He was bruised for our iniquities; upon Him was the chastisement that made us whole, and with His stripes we are healed.*
>
> "*All we like sheep have gone astray; we have turned, every one to his own way; and the Lord has laid on Him the iniquity of us all. He was oppressed, and He was afflicted, yet He opened not His mouth; like a lamb that is led to the slaughter, and like a sheep that before its shearers is dumb, so He opened not His mouth. By oppression and judgment, He was taken away; and as for His generation,*

> *who considered that He was cut off out of the land of the living, stricken for the transgression of my people? And they made His grave with the wicked and with a rich man in His death, although He had done no violence, and there was no deceit in His mouth."* (53:3-9).

And these are words that were amazingly fulfilled as God the Son, the second Persona of the Trinity (see chap.22) was whipped, and beaten, and physically abused, by Roman soldiers, and Temple guards. As He was led to a hill called Calvary, and there fastened by ropes and nails, to a wooden cross, between two convicted criminals. As He was left to suffer, and die – His body pierced with a spear to ensure that death had occurred. As His body was removed, and laid in the tomb of a rich man. And yet He was innocent of any charge brought against Him.

> *"... in Christ God was reconciling the world to Himself, not counting their trespasses against them, and entrusting to us the message of reconciliation. So we are ambassadors for Christ, God making His appeal through us. We beseech you on behalf of Christ, be reconciled to God. For our sake He (the Father) made Him (the Son) to be sin who knew no sin, so that in Him we might become the righteousness of God."* (II Cor.5:19-21).

Yom Kip´pur, the Day of Atonement, is the holiest day of the Jewish year. During the 25-hour period of Yom Kip'pur (from sunset until about an hour past sunset the following day), Jews fulfil the biblical commandment, in Leviticus 16, to fast. Taking neither food nor water, they engage in intense soul-searching and prayer for forgiveness. For almost the entire 25 hours (except for a few hours of sleep at home), Jews are in the synagogue seeking God's forgiveness, and reflecting upon the course of their lives.

One custom associated with the observance of Yom Kippur is the *mikvah*, or "ritual bath" in which Jews immerse themselves. This practice, from which the Christian rite of baptism emerged, symbolizes purification and regeneration, as well as new birth through repentance. It is a reminder of the frailty of human existence, and of our responsibility to act charitably and compassionately toward the less fortunate. The drama of Yom Kippur ends with a blast of the *shofar*, or ram's horn, and the congregation's cry, "Next year in Jerusalem!"

But it was in the unique sacrifice of the Lord Jesus that restoration was accomplished. It is in Him that Father God is able to again have a loving relationship with you and with me. In His humanity, He bore the punishment that we deserved; in His deity, He provided the perfection that alone could satisfy the righteous wrath of the Holy One. Indeed, Paul makes an amazing point when, writing to the early Christian church in Corinth, he says,

> "*For our sake He made Him to be sin who knew no sin, so that in Him we might become the righteousness of God.*" (II Cor.5:21).

Is this why, on the cross, the Son cried out in anguish,

> "*'Eli, Eli, la'ma sabach-tha'ni?'* that is, *'My God, my God, why hast Thou forsaken Me?'*" (Matt 27:46)?

Was it that the Son not only

> "*... bore our sins in His body on the tree*" (I Pet.2:24),

but that He also became, as it were, the very personification of sin! Little wonder that the eyes of the holy Father could not even bear to look upon Him.

The wonderful fact is that He went to that cross; and He died that death; and in doing so, He assured a result - that man might be, once more, at one with His Creator. And this is why the words of John 3:16 must be read carefully!

> "*For God so loved the world, that He gave His only-begotten Son; that whoever believes in Him should not perish, but have eternal life.*"

Did you notice the tense of the verb, just there?

> "*... might **have** eternal life.*"

It's in the present tense! And that means that this eternal life isn't just something that I experience after my physical death (wonderful 'though even that would be!), but something that I experience from the moment of my conversion! I am already living, as it were, in the presence of Almighty God. As the old song says:

"And He walks with me, and He talks with me;
He tells me I am His own.
And the joy we share as we tarry there,
none other has ever known."

Yes, although there is, just now, a veil that separates the heavenly dimension from the dimensions of time and space that are our physical experience, when I am in Christ, I am able to experience a spiritual dimension that enables me to enjoy an intimacy with my Creator that is not available to those who have not yet bowed the knee before Jesus. For many years, I taught that when, at the physical death of the Lord Jesus at Calvary, the veil of the temple was torn in two, from top to bottom, it was symbolic of two things – that it was God Who tore that veil reaching, as it were, down from heaven and gripping it at the top; and that this meant that I no longer needed a priest to represent me before God – I could approach the very throne of grace, myself, in prayer. I still believe that. However, I now go much further. I now believe firmly that the 'barrier' between time and eternity was also torn – a barrier that is much 'thinner' than we may realise – and that my access to the Father is closer than I am able to appreciate; that I may, in and through the Son, enjoy an intimacy that is even greater than that enjoyed by our first human parents in that Garden in Eden! In the atonement, I am truly 'at one' with Him.

Atonement. The act of Almighty God that allows me to be in a relationship with Him that is so close that we may be said to be 'at one'. A restoring of the relationship that was destroyed when Adam and Eve disobeyed, and allowed sin and evil to have free reign on the earth. A restoration that was accomplished through the sacrifice of the Lord Jesus, the Christ – God the Son – when He hung on a Roman cross. But what a result! Because I am at one with my Creator, I enjoy the benefits of His life, here and now. It was the only way; but He took it – for you, and for me.

"Before the stars were hung or planets fashioned,
Before the clay was formed to make a man,
Christ was the Lamb of God for sinners offered --
This was redemption's one and only plan.

"The wealth of all the world could not redeem us,
Nor could our feeble works -- so great the price!
Our only hope is in the blood of Jesus --
The blood He shed for us in sacrifice.

"So, friend, if you would find the way to heaven,
If from the guilt of sin you would be free,
Accept the only way by God provided --
The great redeeming work at Calvary.

"O, I must tell the news where'er He leads me,
Proclaim the Gospel sound both far and near;
The way, the truth, the life is found in Jesus --
This is the message all the world must hear.

Chorus:
"There was no other way a God of love could find
To reconcile the world and save a lost mankind;
It took the death of His own Son upon a tree --
There was no other way but Calvary." (John W. Peterson)

Chapter 7

Procrastination

"Know the true value of time; snatch, seize, and enjoy every moment of it. No idleness; no laziness; no procrastination; never put off 'til tomorrow what you can do today."
(Lord Chesterfield : 1694 – 1773)

Writing in what is now a very (!) old edition of "The Soldier's Armoury" – a system of Bible-reading notes published by The Salvation Army – Major William Clark, a Salvation Army officer, has this to say concerning the Old Testament book of Ruth: "The story of Ruth is beautifully told, and might be read for its own sake, as a delightful story of country life in ancient Palestine. But, as we shall see, the writer had an important purpose in mind when he wrote his book, and the truths he so clearly sets forth are relevant still."

"... the truths he so clearly sets forth are relevant still." How true the Major's words are, not only for the book of Ruth, but for the whole of the Scriptures – this written Word of God which, 'though old, is ever new. In this chapter, I want to suggest that one of the very important lessons that we may learn from the book of Ruth concerns the subject of procrastination – a word that is not solely to do with the Christian faith, but one that has a great bearing on it. The word itself means, quite simply, putting something off until a later time, and it is of great importance when that something is a decision; a decision that effects the life of the individual both in time, and in eternity.

In the book of Ruth, and in the eighteenth verse of chapter three, we find these words of Naomi, concerning her kinsman, Boaz:

"*... the man will not rest, but will settle the matter today.*"

Boaz obviously had the reputation of being a man of action; no procrastinator, at least in the realm of business. And the relevance of those words to you and to me, is that we should not procrastinate in the spiritual realm.

Let's look more closely, then, at this man Boaz, and apply what we learn to our own situation.

The first thing that we learn from this story is that opportunity presents itself. Pre-exilic, middle-eastern, customs regarding courtship and marriage; the perpetuation of

"*... the name of the dead to his inheritance.*" (Ruth 4:5,10);

and the rights of redemption of a next-of-kin; are all strange to our modern, western, minds. Suffice it to say that Boaz was presented with an opportunity to marry Ruth, and to buy the land that had belonged to Elim'elech, Naomi's late husband, from his widow. He didn't go out of his way to bring about the situation that arose; in all likelihood, he had had no prior interest in the land; and, since the strong implication is that he was unmarried, he apparently had had no prior interest in taking to himself a wife. But, unsought and unexpected, the opportunity presented itself.

And, for you and for me, opportunity knocks, as God speaks to us – often when we least expect Him to; sometimes, when we don't particularly want Him to! But He speaks – through circumstances; through the words of Christian friends; through a worship service; through the spoken Word; through the written Word; even through the pages of a book like this. He speaks, as the writer of the Letter to Hebrew disciples of Jesus put it:

"*In many and various ways ...*" (Heb.1:1);

but He speaks! And, as He speaks, He offers you salvation, peace, power. He offers you eternal life in Christ Jesus – a new quality of life that begins here and now, and continues into that eternal dimension in which

"*... there shall be no night ...*" (Rev.21:25);

that timelessness of eternity. (see, further, ch.25).

Opportunity presents itself and, because it does, a decision has to be made. This was certainly the case with Boaz. He couldn't just sit on the fence; he couldn't spend too much time thinking about the situation; he couldn't procrastinate. He had to take action; he had to make a move. There was a kinsman of Naomi who had a closer relationship with her, and he had to be given the opportunity as well. But the matter must be resolved as quickly as possible. And so, as we read on in this beautiful story, we find Boaz setting out, early the next day, spelling out the situation to the next-of-kin, and asking only if he was willing to redeem the land that had belonged to Elim'elech.

Well, this would be material gain; this would be additional wealth; and the next-of-kin had no hesitation.

"*... he said, "I will redeem it.*" (Ruth 4:4).

But then came the catch! Boaz continued:

"*The day you buy the field from the hand of Naomi, you are also buying Ruth the Moabitess, the widow of the dead, in order to restore the name of the dead to his inheritance.*" (Ruth 4:5).

This was a different kettle of fish! The next-of-kin thought again. If he did this, then any offspring of his marriage to Ruth would be entitled to a share of all of his property. If this business was, in the long run, going to see his belongings end up being owned by the children of a Moabitess ...!! Better, by far, to forget the whole thing. And so, through his failure to accept, he rejected.

What a lesson there is here, for us! When the Gospel message is presented to us; when we receive the opportunity of salvation in Christ; we must make a decision. We must accept that offer. We must act as quickly as Boaz did, and we must remember that, as in the case of the next-of-kin, failure to accept means that we have rejected.

An opportunity had presented itself to Boaz; he had made a decision, and acted positively upon it; and so a result was ensured. And, indeed, a result is ensured whether, or not, we act. Boaz went forward, because of the action he took, into a new, and living, relationship of love; a relationship that bore fruit, the full significance of which, he would never have dreamed! The next-of-kin, because he wasn't prepared to make a full commitment; because he wasn't prepared to pay the price; lost all. Indeed, we don't even know his name!

And the same is true of the Gospel message. Those who seize the opportunity – *carpe diem*, to use that old Latin phrase; who decide to follow the Lord, Jesus the Christ; who act, positively, upon that decision; enter into a new life, and a new relationship with Him. Those who fail to accept Him, lose all.

It's a well known saying that 'Procrastination is the thief of time'. However, it might be better said that 'Procrastination is the thief of souls'. How many people go to hell because they put off the matter of their soul's salvation? The old preachers would have said: "Don't put it off 'til tomorrow, because tomorrow never comes". Some might have thought: "Where did they go to school? Tomorrow never comes? That doesn't make sense." But it does! You see, when you keep putting something off until tomorrow, then when tomorrow comes, it becomes today, and then you say: "Well, tomorrow ..." – and then tomorrow it becomes, again, "Tomorrow", and it never becomes "Today". A poet put it like this:

'Tomorrow', he promised his conscience,
'Tomorrow, I mean to believe.
Tomorrow, I'll think as I ought to,
Tomorrow, the Saviour receive.

Tomorrow, I'll conquer the habits
That hold me from Heaven away.'
But ever his conscience repeated
One word, and one only – 'Today!'

Tomorrow! Tomorrow! Tomorrow!
Thus, day after day, it went on.
Tomorrow! Tomorrow! Tomorrow!
'Til youth, like a vision, had gone;

'Til age, and his passions, had written
The message of fate on his brow;
And forth from the shadows came Death,
With the pitiless syllable, 'Now!'" *(Author unknown)*

An opportunity presented – and even as you have read these pages, you have been presented with the opportunity to yield yourself to Jesus, the Christ.

A decision made – and each one of us makes that decision, whether we do so consciously, or not. If we have not, deliberately, and specifically, asked the Christ to take control of our lives then, albeit unconsciously, we have rejected Him.

A result ensured. Those who yield to Him will receive eternal life, here and now, and know the joy and the peace and the pardon and the power that He brings; those who fail to yield to Him will continue on that broad path that leads to destruction.

It was said of Boaz,

> "... *the man will not rest, but will settle the matter today.*"

His was a matter of a physical relationship. But the far more important matter that faces each one of us concerns a spiritual relationship.

> "*Behold, now is the acceptable time; behold, now is the day of salvation.*" (II Cor. 6:2).

Do not rest; settle it right now. Tomorrow may be too late!

Chapter 8

GRACE

"Grace, grace, God's grace
Grace that is greater than all our sin"

When the well-known American evangelist, Billy Graham, was driving through a small southern town, he was stopped by a policeman and charged with speeding. Dr. Graham admitted his guilt, but was told by the officer that he would have to appear in court.

The judge asked, "Guilty, or not guilty?" When the preacher pleaded guilty, the judge replied, "That'll be ten dollars – a dollar for every mile you went over the limit."

Then, suddenly the judge recognized the famous evangelist. "You have violated the law," he said. "The fine must be paid – but I am going to pay it for you." He took a ten-dollar bill from his own wallet, attached it to the ticket, and then took Graham out and bought him a steak dinner! "That," said Billy Graham, when he recounted the story, "is how God treats **repentant** sinners!"

And that is grace.

Grace is a word that is not unfamiliar to most people. Even in the 21st century, there are those who will "say grace" either before or after a meal – giving thanks to God for His provision. Within the Episcopal denominations (the Church of England; the Church of

Rome), and within the British (English?!) aristocracy, "Your Grace" is the proper salutation for those of a particular "rank/standing".

But grace, as a great word of the Christian faith, is something else.

On holiday in France, one summer, my wife and I had unexpected access to the internet because of the generosity of a young man at the camp-site at which we had just arrived, in the town of Albi – north-east of Toulouse. We had noticed him, carrying a laptop, as we arrived and, as we were erecting the awning on the caravan, he walked by. I excused myself and, explaining that we had noticed his laptop, asked if a wireless network was available on the site. He informed me that, unfortunately, there was not, and I indicated that that was okay. "However", he continued (in French, of course!!) "I have a solution." That solution was very simple. He would let me use his own internet 'dongle' – a device (for the uninitiated!) that allows internet access directly from a satellite, at a cost. I thanked him, and enquired as to what I would have to pay. "Rien", was the instant response – "Nothing".

He arrived, shortly afterwards, complete with dongle, and even sat and ensured that it was correctly installed, as all of the on-screen instructions were in French! As we chatted, I discovered that he came from the town of Besançon, and that he was in his second year of a degree course in mechanical science (if my memory serves me well!). I continued to practice my French with him, while he practised his English language skills with me. It was good, then, to have some time online just to clear out a load of spam, and check some more important e-mails – as well as some newspaper headlines from the UK!

The one thing that I haven't mentioned is that the young man was an obviously devout Muslim. My wife brought him a glass of Pepsi and, although he expressed his gratitude – it was a very warm day –

he checked with me, before drinking, that it did not contain alcohol. His name (sadly forgotten) was an obviously Arabic one, and his skin tone indicated a Middle Eastern, rather than a European, background.

A few days later, we surprised some friends (whom I will not name, in order to avoid any possible embarrassment) who were staying at a camp-site that was costing more than twice as much as we were paying where we were camped. We could barely believe our ears when they suggested that we move to their site – and they would pay half of our costs! This would have cost them something in the region of £100.00 – just for the pleasure of our company for a few nights. This is a family who would claim to be totally secular, if not atheistic.

What we witnessed on those two occasions was undeserved, unnecessary, and totally unexpected. And that is also a way (or ought I to say 'another two ways'?!) by which we may illustrate the grace of God. We had done nothing that could have given us the right to demand such generosity – and not one of us has ever done anything that would entitle us to God's grace. Neither our young Muslim friend, nor our secular friends of longer standing, were under any obligation to treat us in the generous ways that they did – and the Almighty Creator of all that is certainly isn't under any obligation to sinful mortals like us. We were wonderfully surprised by the generosity that these dear people showed to us – and we are constantly amazed at the ways in which God shows His grace towards us.

By the way, we also wondered just how many of our Christian friends would treat us in such ways – and, more pertinently, how ready we would be to treat others in such a way!!

> "... whenever we have the opportunity, we should do good to everyone – especially to those in the family of faith." (Gal.6:10).

Not for the first (or the last!) time, we learned from our unconverted friends!

We accepted the offer from our young Muslim friend; the other (even more generous) offer, we declined. This was not intended as a slight to our friends, whose generosity was, is, and always will be, appreciated more than we can say – and we truly hoped that we didn't offend them in any way. There were other, personal, reasons, for our not accepting it. But the simple fact remains that we didn't and they, of course, were unable to force us to do so.

The grace of God is offered to one and all. But if we don't respond, positively, to that offer – the generosity of which is beyond measure – then He will not force it upon us. The ultimate choice is always ours. However, although declining our friends' offer meant that we lost out on a few pleasant evenings together, enjoying each other's company and 'bonhomie'; declining the offer of full salvation through the grace of God, means eternity banished from His glorious Presence. How sad that so many deliberately decide to do so.

It is a sad fact of life that slavery – abolished in Great Britain in 1807 after years of campaigning in Parliament by William Wilberforce and others; men who were driven by their Christian faith and beliefs – continues in the world today, under the euphemistic term of 'human trafficking'. Indeed, it has been estimated that there are more slaves today – working in conditions that most of us could barely imagine, let alone understand – than there were in the four centuries of slavery that preceded Wilberforce's great work. Towards the end of that same year,

1807, died one, Rev. John Newton, author of the well-known song "Amazing Grace".

Newton, of course, had been captain of a slave ship, plying his trade between the west coast of the African continent, and the new world of North America and the Caribbean islands. But, on May 10th, 1748, he was soundly converted and eventually became an Anglican clergyman, faithfully preaching the Gospel of the grace of God, displayed in the Lord, Jesus Christ, right up until the last year of his earthly life.

Commenting on the word 'grace', as it is found in Paul's letter to the believing people in Ephesus, William Hendriksen writes: "This word ... refers undoubtedly to **God's spontaneous, unmerited, favour in action; His freely-bestowed loving-kindness in operation; bestowing salvation upon guilt-laden sinners.**" (Commentary, in loc; *emphasis added*)

The most important thing to note, of course, is that grace is God's. It is of and from Him, and only He can bestow it. And the other preliminary point that must be emphasised is that we don't deserve it! It is a spontaneous and unmerited act of God; we cannot demand it as our right; it is the product of God's own love.

But having made those general, and introductory, remarks about this amazing grace, I want to look with you at grace itself. And the first thing that we may note, and in which we may rejoice, is that grace is without cost.

It comes to us entirely free of charge. Not that it is worthless! Far from it; indeed, it is valuable beyond anything that you or I could ever pay! But the price has already been paid by someone else. And that Someone is the Lord Jesus Himself.

I recall once, being asked by my younger daughter if I would accompany her to a local car dealership, as she wanted to purchase a newer car than the one she had. Naturally, I agreed to go with her – although I was really little more than 'moral support'! Having spent some time looking at various models, noting the mileage, the condition, the specification and, most importantly, the price, she sat down with a salesman in order to make the financial arrangements to pay for the car that she had chosen. So many possibilities – each with its own attraction! This plan meant a shorter time to have to make monthly payments – but the payments were more than she could afford. That plan meant quite small payments – but she would still be paying for the car after it had gone to the scrap-yard! Another plan was just outside her budget, but it did include comprehensive breakdown cover so that she would never need to be stuck anywhere with a car that was going nowhere. It wasn't an easy choice but, eventually, a decision was made and my daughter was the owner of a much newer car. But just imagine … …!

Imagine that the Sales Manager had come over to her and had handed her a set of keys. And imagine that he had informed her that they were the keys to a brand new, top of the range model of the car that she wanted. And imagine, if you can (!), that he went on to tell her that it was covered for all of its servicing, insurance, weekly valeting, and fuel, for as long as she had it – and that it would cost her absolutely nothing; that some anonymous benefactor had paid, up front, enough to cover all of that! Well after she had been picked up from the floor, and supplied with an oxygen mask to aid her recovery, she would have been overjoyed!

But that is, in reality, a picture of grace. Paid for in full by Jesus so that you and I might receive it, free of charge. When He hung on that cross, and just before He gave up His spirit, He uttered a loud shout – and it **was** a loud shout that must have startled those who were standing around. In Greek, it is just one word:

"Tetelestai!"

It means 'Finished'. He had completed the task that the Father had given Him. He had paid the price, in full, for your sin and mine. "The price is paid!" we sometimes sing, "Come, let us enter in to all that Jesus died to make our own. For every sin, more than enough He gave, and bought our freedom from each guilty stain." (Graham Kendrick)

It has been said that the easiest way to remember what grace is, is to use the acrostic **G**od's **R**iches **A**t **C**hrist's **E**xpense. All that God has, and is, can be mine, by His grace, because Jesus has paid the price.

In his letter to the disciples of Jesus in Ephesus, Paul writes

"... *by grace you have been saved, through faith; and this is not your own doing, it is the gift of God – not because of works, lest any man should boast.*" (2:8).

And so we learn that salvation comes by grace – it is God's free, unmerited gift. And if we were to go through the Scriptures fully, we would discover that many other things are bound up in grace – forgiveness, deliverance from the power and penalty of sin, justification, and the list could go on. All offered to you and to me without cost; all offered as God's gracious gift; all bound up in His grace.

It's without cost; and it's without condition. Amazingly, God doesn't even set out conditions that have to be met before He bestows His grace upon us! As we accept Him, and the gifts of His grace, we do find that there **are** conditions attached – but these are more of a necessary response to His love than a prerequisite to receiving it. Faith, at which we looked in the first chapter, is the prime response. But even if we have no faith, the offer is still made.

I've already shared the idea of my daughter receiving, at no cost to her, a brand-new car, with the assurance that it is even going to be kept for her. Fuel, oil, servicing charges, weekly valet, road tax, insurance, all going to be paid for. And, says her anonymous benefactor, there are no conditions attached to the offer.

But if she is unable to drive, then there is, in fact, a condition attached – that she learn to do so, and pass her driving test! Otherwise, the gift, exceptional 'though it is, is totally useless to her.

The grace of God is offered in a similar manner. But the fact that certain conditions will have to be met if I do appropriate the offer, doesn't affect the fact that the offer itself is without condition.

Without cost; without condition; and without compare. Paul, when leaving Ephesus during his third missionary journey, was able to say to the elders,

> *"And now, I commend you to God, and to the work of His grace, that is able to build you up, and to give you an inheritance among all those who are sanctified."* (Acts 20:28).

It is only by the grace of God that we can be built up spiritually; it is only by His grace that we can receive the inheritance of His children. Incomparable grace – without compare in its make-up; and without compare in its measure.

In the eighth chapter of John's account of the Gospel, is the lovely story of the woman who, it was alleged, had been taken in the very act of adultery. This woman was brought before the Lord Jesus, by a group of

"... *teachers of religious law, and Pharisees, as He taught in the Temple.*" (v.2).

She was placed in front of the crowd – ashamed, humiliated, an object of scorn – and the question was put to the Master:

"*The law of Moses says to stone her. What do You say?*" (v.5).

John explains that this was not an attempt to uphold the law on adultery. Rather

"*They were trying to trap Him into saying something they could use against Him, ...*" (v.6).

They knew what they were doing. Now they had Him – this One Who constantly showed them up for the hypocrites they undoubtedly were. If He agreed that she should be stoned, His reputation for being a Man of mercy would be destroyed. Furthermore, they could get Him into serious trouble with the Roman authorities, as only they had the right to sentence to death. However, if He said that she should be released, then He would be shown, clearly, to have no regard for the Law of Moses – and His reputation as a Teacher would then be destroyed. Either way, they had Him – or so they thought!

The Master's response was, to say the least, unusual! He

"*...stooped down and wrote in the dust with his finger.*" (v.8).

What did He write? The Holy Spirit has not seen fit to reveal that to us. However, could it be that He wrote words such as 'adultery', 'murder', 'stealing', 'covetousness', 'anger', 'idolatry'? Words gleaned straight from the Ten Commandments (the Ten Words) that these religious men claimed to defend!

John records:

> "*They kept demanding an answer, so He stood up again and said, 'All right, stone her. But let those who have never sinned throw the first stones.'*" (v.7).

The result was that they slunk away – beginning with the oldest who, we may safely presume, were most guilty – until only Jesus and the woman were left standing in the middle of the crowd.

> "*'Where are your accusers?', He asked her. 'Didn't even one of them condemn you?' 'No, Lord,' she said. And Jesus said, 'Neither do I. Go **and sin no more**.*'" (vs.10-11; *emphasis added*).

An act of incomparable grace.

Writing to his son in the faith, Timothy, Paul states that

> "*… the grace of our Lord overflowed for me with the faith and love that are in Christ Jesus.*" "*… the grace of our Lord overflowed …*" (ITim.1:14).

That's grace beyond measure!

And it's without compare in its motive. Why is such grace given to us? Paul answers the question in his letter to the Corinthian believers:

> "*For it is all for your sake, so that as grace extends to more and more people, it may increase thanksgiving, to the glory of God.*" (II Cor.4:15).

Paul is speaking, here, of his ministry among the Gentiles. That ministry was all for their sake, that the grace of God might abound among them. And that, in turn, thanksgiving to God might be increased, and His Name be glorified.

Those of a certain age, and ecclesiastical background, may remember the first question in the Westminster Shorter Catechism? "What is the chief end (the prime purpose, the 'raison d'être') of man?" And the answer? "Man's chief end is to glorify God, and to enjoy Him for ever." There can be no greater motive then the glory of God.

If the Christian life does not begin with an experience of the grace of God, it has no real beginning; but if it does begin with grace, then there is no end to its growth, and adventure. It's the grace of God at work within us that melts our cold self-assertiveness, and astounds us that we are loved in spite of what we have been and done. It was so for Paul – and it continues to be so today for all who call on the Name of Jesus. As we've already noted, it's what happened to John Newton when that unchanging love broke into his wild, vagabond life. After years of rebellion and resistance, he was captured – by grace. Listen to a little bit of his own testimony:

"In evil, long I took delight, un-awed by shame and fear;
'Til a new object struck my sight, and stopped my wild career.
Amazing grace!
How sweet the sound that saved a wretch like me!
I once was lost, but now I'm found; was blind, but now I see."

Grace – without cost; without condition; without compare. Grace: God's own gift to undeserving sinners. Grace: the general experience of each one of us, even if we haven't been aware of it.

When a person works an eight-hour day, and receives a fair day's pay for his time, that is a wage. When a person competes with an opponent, and receives a trophy for his performance, that is a prize. When a person receives appropriate recognition for his long service, or high achievements, that is an award. But when a person is not capable of earning a wage, can win no prize, and deserves no award – yet receives such a gift anyway – that is a good picture of

God's unmerited favour. This is what we mean when we talk about the grace of God.

May God grant to each one of us, by His grace, the courage, and strength, and faith, to respond positively to it, that we might appropriate all of its wonderful blessings and benefits at a personal level; and be found, in the company of all of His faithful people, giving all of the glory to Him.

Chapter 9

REDEMPTION

"In Him we have redemption through His blood, the forgiveness of our trespasses, according to the riches of His grace which He lavished upon us." (Ephesians 1:7-8)

When the words at which we are looking were first used, most of them were words of common, everyday, speech; easily understood by the most illiterate peasant. And the word at which we look in this chapter is a word that was especially well-understood in a slave-ridden society – the word 'redemption'.

Basically, the word means "deliverance from some evil, by payment of a price." It is more than simple deliverance. Thus prisoners-of-war might be released on payment of a price, that was called a 'ransom', and they were said to have been redeemed. And, of course, the more important the prisoner, the greater the sum demanded – leading to the description of a very large sum of money as "a king's ransom"; i.e. a sum large enough to pay for the redemption of a king.

I still recall the pawn-shop at the corner of the street in which my maternal grandmother lived. Today, it might well be called "Cash Converters". The idea behind a pawn-shop was that if a working man was short of cash towards the end of the week, he could take some item of value to the pawn-shop, where the pawnbroker would give him a sum of money for it. The worker would receive a receipt for the item and then, when he was paid his wages, he could buy it back – at a higher price, of course, than what he had received for it. And he was said to have redeemed it.

Again, a slave might be released by a process of ransom. What happened here was that the slave somehow saved up the price of his freedom; went to the temple of whatever 'god' he chose; and paid the price to the 'god' – or, at least, to the priest as the representative of the 'god'. As far as men were concerned he was, from that moment on, a free man but, technically, he was considered to be the slave of the 'god', and certain religious obligations might be laid upon him.

It is this concept that is behind the Christian use of the word 'redemption' and, coupled to it, is an Old Testament idea – that of the *go-el*, or kinsman, whose duty it was, amongst others (such as wreaking vengeance; and assuring the practice of Levirate marriage, cf. Ruth and Boaz; ch.7) to redeem the property of a fellow-kinsman who had fallen into the hands of creditors.

You and I are slaves – slaves to sin; we are in the hands of a creditor – even the satan (adversary). And we need to be redeemed! But we have a problem. You see, unlike the slave of a human master, we can never save up, or gain in any way, for ourselves, a satisfactory price to be freed from sin. We may attempt to do all sorts of good works; we may seek, earnestly, to think only pure and lovely thoughts; we may even, as Paul put it in another context,

> "*give away all that [we] have, and … deliver our bodies to be burned, …*" (I Cor.13:3);

but none of this is enough. For, at heart, we are still sinners – and there's nothing that we can do about it, by ourselves.

And so, we need another to redeem us. But, again, there is a problem. For no other mortal is able to do this for another. Therefore, we need Someone greater than we are to redeem us – to be our **go-el**, our kinsman. Praise God that He provided that Someone in the Persona of the only-begotten Son.

With all of this in mind, let's consider just three things about the redemption of which Paul speaks in Ephesians 1:7 where, writing to disciples of Jesus, he says:

"*In [Jesus] we have redemption through His blood ...*"

Let's think, first of all, on the cost of, or the price that had to be paid for, our redemption. That's the first thing that we noticed about the slave – he had to pay a price. The price involved would be decided by the slave's importance to his master – that is to say that a slave who was a schoolteacher to his master's children would have a much higher redemption-price than a kitchen-maid. It's really quite straightforward. The more important one person is to another, the more he is prepared to pay for him; the higher the value that is placed on the other's life.

It is highly unlikely that my wife, or either of my daughters, or my grandson, will ever be kidnapped. I am neither rich enough, nor influential enough, to make it worth anyone's while. But if I had a million pounds in the bank, and one, or all, of them were kidnapped, I would gladly give over every last penny to ensure their safety – they're much too important to me to do otherwise. Indeed, if it came to it, I can say that I would even lay down my own life for them. What loving husband, father, or grandfather, would do otherwise?

The ransom for you and for me; the price paid for our redemption; was nothing less than the blood of Jesus. We are so important to Almighty God that, in the Persona of the Son, He laid down His own life for us. He loves us so much that He hung on a cross for us, suffering pain and anguish, the like of which we may never experience!

> "... *He was wounded and crushed for our sins;*
> *He was beaten that we might have peace;*
> *With the stripes that wounded Him,*
> *we are healed and made whole.*" (Isaiah 53:5).

"There was no other good enough
to pay the price of sin.
He only [*i.e. He alone*], could unlock the gates
of heaven, and let us in."   (Cecil Frances Alexander)

What a cost! What a 'king's ransom'! And it was paid, freely and fully, for you and for me.

> "*In [Jesus], we have redemption, through His blood ...*"

But let's move on, and consider the claim. Remember what was said above – that the slave, once the ransom was paid, was free as far as other men were concerned; that he was free as far as his previous owner was concerned; but that, technically, he was now the slave of the 'god' to whom the ransom had been paid. That is to say, the 'god' had a claim upon the slave's life!

So it is in the act of redemption through the blood of the Christ. As He has redeemed us, God has a claim upon us. The well-known (to those of a certain age!) story of John's boat illustrates this well. John was a creative child. One day, he found a piece of wood and, with his trusty pocket-knife (this was also before the days of suffocation by Health & Safety!), he started to whittle away at it until he eventually fashioned a lovely boat. Every day, he would take it down to the local river, and he would watch with some pride as his boat sailed so beautifully in the water. One day, however, the river was flowing so quickly that the boat was carried away before John could catch hold of it.

John was very sad. He reckoned that he would never see his beloved boat again.

Some weeks later, John's mother took him with her to the nearby town. They visited a number of shops as his mother made different purchases. Then as they walked past the big toy-shop, John stopped. There, in the window, was something that he immediately recognised. It was his boat; the very boat on which he had lavished such care as he shaped it, and added the superstructure; the boat that he had last seen disappearing from view in the rapid flow of the river. There was a price tag on the boat. John reached into his pocket, and pulled out the cash that was there. It was going to take every penny – but he did have just enough to pay for the boat. He went into the shop, handed over his money, and walked out with the boat in his arms. Looking down at it he said: "Ye're twice mine. A wrocht ye, an' a bocht ye!" "You're twice mine. I made you, and I paid the price for you." What a claim John had to his boat!

And that's the claim that Almighty God has on each one of us. "You're twice mine", He says. "I created you and, when you were lost in sin, I paid the price for you – I redeemed you!"

And so, when He speaks into my life, He is not simply making a polite request; He is issuing a command. When I act upon what He says, I am not doing Him some kind of favour; I am merely displaying the obedience that is His rightful due. (see Luke 17:10).

This leads us on to the third aspect of redemption in the Christian faith, which is the contract.

The slave, when redeemed, was the slave of the 'god' and, we learned, certain religious, or pious, obligations might be laid upon him. This is actually where the analogy breaks down. For, in the case of redemption through the blood of the Lord Jesus, there is no concept of 'might'! Obligations are laid upon the redeemed of Christ. Those who are redeemed in Him are called to live their lives in a certain way; they are called to respond to His love with the love of their own hearts; they are called to acknowledge Him, publicly and continually, as Saviour and Lord; they are called to commitment – everything they have, and everything they are, given over to His control. They are, in fact, called to a new slavery – and the apostles glory in the title of "slave (*doulos*) of the Lord, Jesus Christ" (Rom.1:1; I Cor.7:21; Gal.1:10; James 1:1; II Pet.1:1; Jude 1:1; Rev.1:1) – but a slavery in which, alone, is found real freedom.

"Make me a captive, Lord;
and then I shall be free.
Force me to render up my sword,
and I shall conqueror be."   (George Matheson)

Redemption – the cost: the very blood of Jesus;
              the claim: we belong to God;
              the contract: He demands our total commitment

There's just one more thing that must be emphasised. You see, if I have been kidnapped, and my family pay the ransom that is being demanded, but I refuse to leave my captors; then my family, while showing their deep love for me, have wasted their time, effort, and money.

If someone paid the redemption-price on behalf of a slave, and the slave refused to accept the offer, he remained in his state of enslavement. If a condemned man, in the death-cell, is told that someone else has offered to bear the punishment for his crime, but refuses to accept the offer – or even just ignores it – he still has that death penalty executed upon him.

What I'm trying to emphasise is simply that an offer must be accepted if it is to be of any use. And this is the tragedy of mankind: not that it is sinful; not that every one of us is born a sinner; but that so many reject, or fail to accept, or totally ignore, the offer of salvation – of redemption from the power of the devil, made possible through that sacrifice of the Lord Jesus at Calvary.

John, in the Revelation, speaks of those who

> "...have been **redeemed** from mankind as first fruits for God and the Lamb, ..." (14:4); and Isaiah, prophesying hundreds of years earlier, looks to the day when "*The wilderness and the dry land shall be glad, the desert shall rejoice and blossom; like the crocus it shall blossom abundantly, and rejoice with joy and singing. ... ... And a highway shall be there, and it shall be called the Holy Way; the unclean shall not pass over it, and fools shall not err therein. No lion shall be there, nor shall any ravenous beast come up on it; they shall not be found there, but the* **redeemed** *shall walk there. And the ransomed of YHWH shall return, and come to Zion with singing; everlasting joy shall be upon their heads; they shall obtain joy and gladness, and sorrow and sighing shall flee away.*" (35: 1-2[a], 8-10).

The exhortation of the Psalmist is:

> "*O give thanks to YHWH, for He is good; for His steadfast love endures for ever! Let the* **redeemed** *of YHWH say so, whom He has* **redeemed** *from trouble ...*" (107:1-2).

Have you accepted, for yourself, this wonderful redemption, gained at such great cost? Have you acknowledged God's double claim upon your life? Have you committed yourself to Him – body, mind, and spirit – in an eternal contract? If you haven't, then I urge you to do so right now – acting upon the knowledge that is now yours. If you have, then tell others of the goodness, and the greatness; the love, and the power; of the Lord, your strength – and your Redeemer.

Chapter 10

THE KINGDOM OF GOD

"My Kingdom is not of this world" (John 18:36)

Whenever I go abroad on holiday, I carry with me a very important document. It's a passport – a British passport – and the name inside is mine. That passport is proof that I am a British subject; a 'citizen' of the United Kingdom of Great Britain and Northern Ireland. One of my sisters-in-law has dual citizenship. She has a Canadian passport as well as a British one – able to be legally resident in either country.

But although I don't, like my sister-in-law, have an additional passport to show and to prove my claim, I hold dual citizenship as well. Because Paul, writing to the Philippian church, and speaking to believers in every age, says:

"We ... are citizens of heaven." (3:20).

So, as a disciple of Jesus, born again of the Spirit of God, I am not only a 'citizen' of the United Kingdom; I am also a citizen of the Kingdom of God (Kingdom of heaven in Matthew's account of the Gospel, showing his strong Jewish belief that the word 'God' ought not to be spoken or written).

In this chapter we are going to consider that Kingdom – a Kingdom that is not marked out by physical boundaries, but that is composed of people: people who have voluntarily submitted themselves to the Kingship of Almighty God. Consider, first of all what the Kingdom of God is like. We need to follow two lines of thought here. Think, first of all, of what it is like in its growth.

Jesus, Himself, likened it to a mustard-seed, or a pinch of yeast. He spoke of it as something that grows silently, and unseen. Just as the seed that is in the earth doesn't grow with a flourish of trumpets, or with the sound of a mighty organ, but just grows on, day by day, unseen for so long; so the Kingdom of God grows, ceaselessly, day by day, often unseen, and unrecognised, by those around.

As we look around at our own nation today, we may find it difficult to believe that the Kingdom of God is growing. Political spin, and political correctness; church buildings being closed for lack of support, while public houses offer longer opening hours; drug addiction and sexual immorality accepted as the norm, and condoned by legislation. Indeed, the whole world seems to be in a state of political and social chaos.

But all of this foretold by the Lord Jesus.

> *"Then He put another parable before them. 'The Kingdom of Heaven,' He said, 'is like a man who sowed good seed in his field. But while his men were asleep, his enemy came and sowed weeds among the wheat, and went away. When the crop came up and ripened, the weeds appeared as well. Then the owner's servants came up to him and said, 'Sir, didn't you sow good seed in your field? Where did all these weeds come from?' 'Some blackguard has done this to spite me,' he replied. 'Do you want us, then, to go out and pull them all up?', asked the servants. 'No!' he answered. 'If you pull up the weeds now, you would pull up the wheat with them. Let them both grow together 'til the harvest. At harvest-time, I shall tell the reapers to*

collect the weeds first, and tie them in bundles, ready to burn; but to collect the wheat, and store it in my barn.'" (Matt.13:24-30)

You see, although the weeds are growing, at a fast and furious rate; although, indeed, they appear at times to be all that is growing; for those with discerning eyes, who know what it is they are looking for, the wheat is growing as well. I look at the church in those lands in which to become a Christian is to invite persecution, imprisonment, torture, death. I look at young people going out on short-term missionary activity. From GLO (Gospel Literature Outreach) in Motherwell alone, teams go out in the summer months to an amazing number of locations throughout the British Isles, mainland Europe, and beyond. I look at the work of organisations such as CARE and World Vision, helping the disadvantaged in both this country and in the developing world, all in the Name of the Lord Jesus. And I see much wheat growing amongst the weeds of materialism, and consumerism, and terrorism, and sexual perversion, and anarchy, and lack of proper discipline, and all the rest.

And when the harvest-time comes, and the Son of God returns to this earthly dimension, in all His glory and power, then will the weeds – the evil in this world – be gathered up and burned; while the wheat will be taken into His barn.

In its growth, the Kingdom of God is like a little seed, planted in the ground – silent, ceaseless, certain. What it is like in its growth; and what it is like in its grandeur.

This, for you and me, is something that is largely in the future, as it is only then, when His Kingdom has fully come, or when we ourselves pass through that veil that we call death, that we will see it in all of that grandeur.

But we may catch a glimpse of glory of God's Kingdom even now and, to do so, we turn to the book of the Revelation of the Lord Jesus Christ given to John. There we read about the coming the Kingdom, after the devil has been cast into the lake of fire (12:10). And we find it likened to a city – a new Jerusalem – that is unsurpassed in its beauty and splendour (21:9 – 22:5). We are told that:

> "One of the seven angels who had the seven bowls full of the seven last plagues came and said to me, 'Come, I will show you the bride, the wife of the Lamb.' And he carried me away in the Spirit to a mountain great and high, and showed me the Holy City, Jerusalem, coming down out of heaven from God. It shone with the glory of God, and its brilliance was like that of a very precious jewel, like a jasper, clear as crystal. It had a great, high wall with twelve gates, and with twelve angels at the gates. On the gates were written the names of the twelve tribes of Israel. ... The wall of the city had twelve foundations, and on them were the names of the twelve apostles of the Lamb. ... The wall was made of jasper, and the city of pure gold, as pure as glass. The foundations of the city walls were decorated with every kind of precious stone. The first foundation was jasper, the second sapphire, the third chalcedony, the fourth emerald, the fifth onyx, the sixth carnelian, the seventh chrysolite, the eighth beryl, the ninth topaz, the tenth chrysoprase, the eleventh jacinth, and the twelfth amethyst. The twelve gates were twelve pearls, each gate made of a single pearl. The great street of the city was of pure gold, like transparent glass. I did not see a temple in the city, because the Lord God Almighty and the Lamb are its temple. The city does not need the sun or the moon to shine on it, for the glory of God gives it light, and the Lamb is its lamp. ... Nothing impure will ever enter it, nor

will anyone who does what is shameful or deceitful, but only those whose names are written in the Lamb's book of life.

Then the angel showed me the river of the water of life, as clear as crystal, flowing from the throne of God and of the Lamb down the middle of the great street of the city. On each side of the river stood the tree of life, bearing twelve crops of fruit, yielding its fruit every month. And the leaves of the tree are for the healing of the nations. No longer will there be any curse. The throne of God and of the Lamb will be in the city, and his servants will serve him. They will see his face, and his name will be on their foreheads. There will be no more night. They will not need the light of a lamp or the light of the sun, for the Lord God will give them light. And they will reign for ever and ever." (NIV).

"Nought that defileth," says the old hymn, "Nought that defileth, shall ever enter in."

What the Kingdom of God is like in its growth – silent, ceaseless, certain; and in its grandeur – beautiful and pure.

But we need also to consider where the Kingdom of God is found.

First of all, as has already been already hinted, it is found in the heavenly realms

Turning, again, to the book of the Revelation given to John, we read of the adoration of the Lamb by the four living creatures, and the elders:

"You are worthy to take the scroll and break its seals and open it; for you were slain, and your blood has bought people from every nation as gifts for God. And you have

93

> *gathered them into a kingdom and made them priests of our God; they shall reign upon the earth."* (5:9-10; TLB).

And, later we hear the song of the saints of God:

> *"Great and marvellous are Your doings, Lord God Almighty. Just and true are Your ways, O King of Ages."* (15:3; TLB).
> *"Praise the Lord! For the Lord our God, the Almighty, reigns."* (19:6; TLB)

But it is not only heavenly beings who can praise and adore the King of kings. It is not only in the heavenly realm that His Kingdom is found. Because the Kingdom of God is also found in the human heart.

The Kingdom of God is, in a different sense, already here on earth – in the hearts of those who own Him as King in their lives. An earthly kingdom is not only a geographical area, it is also the area in which a monarch reigns; in which he is supreme. And just as God reigns in heaven, so He reigns in the lives of those who have opened their hearts to Him, and welcomed Him in; those who are willing to say 'Your will be done' – and mean it! One of the hallmarks of the Kingdom of God is, indeed, obedience.

What God's kingdom is like:
> in its growth – silent, ceaseless, certain;
> in its grandeur – beautiful and pure.

Where God's Kingdom is found:
> in the heavenly realms;
> in the human heart.

The third line of thought that we must follow, because it's the most important, concerns how the Kingdom of God is entered. How do we become subjects of the King of kings? Jesus' words to Nicodemus were:

> *"I tell you the truth, no-one can enter the kingdom of God unless he is born of water and the Spirit."* (John 3:5; NIV),

and this spiritual rebirth involves two things.

First of all, there is an acceptance we must make – the acceptance of Jesus as Saviour. It doesn't matter who or what you are; it doesn't matter what colour your skin is; it doesn't matter what your cultural, or educational, background is – entry to the Kingdom of God is through Jesus alone.

You may be a long-standing member of a fellowship/congregation – but this will not gain you entry; you may give generously, even sacrificially, to the work of the church – but this will not gain you entry; you may live an almost perfect, morally-upright life – but this will not gain you entry.

"I am the Way",

said Jesus;

"I am the Door" (Jn.14:6).

Not just any old way, or any old door, but the only way, and the only door.

One of the old choruses, with their greater emphasis on sound theology than some of their modern counterparts, put it like this:

"There's a way back to God from the dark paths of sin;
There's a door that is opened, and you may go in.
At Calvary's cross is where you begin
When you come, as a sinner, to Jesus."

And that's what hurts. We, who live in an age, and a culture, in which much store is put by self-sufficiency; the self-made man; the cult of independency; are loathe to admit that there are some things that we cannot do for ourselves; we are unwilling to come to someone else and admit our need. Yet this is exactly what we must do. We must come, acknowledging our own sinfulness, our own helplessness, and His complete sufficiency. We must come, accepting Him as Saviour.

There is an acceptance we must make; and

Secondly, there is an allegiance we must give.

There are many "half-baked" Christians in the world today – especially in the free and affluent West. They are those who claim to have accepted Christ as Saviour, but who have not given Him complete control of their lives. Always, there is one area that is closed off to Him; one corner of their hearts that He is not allowed to enter. But if we are to be true subjects of the King, and true citizens of His Kingdom, then we must offer our all to Him. God doesn't want just half-hearted citizens in His Kingdom – He wants those whom He can use in His service. He isn't as interested in your ability as he is in your availability!

So we must not only ask the Lord Jesus into our hearts as Saviour; we must also give Him complete control of our lives, as Lord. And if we have entered God's Kingdom through acceptance of His Son as Saviour and Lord, and have offered ourselves as "living sacrifices", then He will be able to use us to advance His Kingdom, here on earth.

Many years ago, the phrase "God's alternative society" was in vogue. The Christian is already a member of that alternative society; a citizen of the Kingdom of God:

A Kingdom that is silent, ceaseless, certain, in its growth; that is beautiful and pure in its grandeur.

A Kingdom that is found in the heavenly realms; and also in the human heart.

A Kingdom that is entered through acceptance of the Lord Jesus as Saviour; and allegiance to Him as King.

I'm glad that I have a British passport; I'm content to be a subject of H.M. the Queen. But it thrills me much more to know that I am a citizen of the Kingdom of God; a subject - and also a child! - of the King of kings.

I wonder – do you have that dual-citizenship? And if you haven't, don't you think it's time you did something about it? Don't you?!

Chapter 11

JUSTIFICATION

"Justification is a judicial act of God, in which He declares, on the basis of the righteousness of Jesus Christ, that all the claims of the law are satisfied with respect to the sinner." (Louis Berkhof)

The great preacher and Biblical expositor of a former generation, Dr Campbell Morgan, in a book entitled "The answers of Jesus to Job" shows, for the Biblical book of that name, the way in which many of the questions of the O.T. are answered, by God, only in Jesus, and in the pages of the N.T.

In this chapter, I want to look at one question asked, centuries – indeed millennia – ago by that same Job; a question echoed by human hearts ever since.

That question is

"How can a mortal man be justified (accounted as righteous), before God?" (9:2)

and, in the 24th verse of the 3rd chapter of Paul's great letter to the infant church at Rome, we find some guidelines to the answer to that timeless question. Commencing with the previous verse, we read:

> "... *since all have sinned and fall short of the glory of God, they are justified by His grace as a gift, through the redemption which is in Christ Jesus, ...*".

Let's look, then, first of all at the word 'justification', and try to discover what it means.

It's not to do with evenly-spaced margins down the sides of a printed page! Nor is it to do with trying to excuse myself for something. It's one of the key-words of this letter to the early Roman disciples of Jesus, where it's found about 50 times, indicating that Paul considered it to be a fairly important concept! The New Bible Dictionary gives the following definition: "God's act of remitting the sins of guilty men [and women!], and accounting them righteous, freely by His grace, through faith in Christ; on the ground, not of their own works, but of the representative law-keeping, and redemptive blood-shedding, of the Lord, Jesus Christ, on their behalf." (*in loc*)

Now, I know that that is an awful lot to digest in just one reading. But the important thing to grasp is perfectly simple. It is that justification, like grace, and salvation, is 'God's act', not man's! It is something that we cannot do for ourselves; something that only God can do for us.

And there are no degrees of justification – either I am justified, or I am not justified. It's a bit like being pregnant! A female either is, or isn't. There is no possibility of being 'just a wee bit' pregnant!

Justification is the central point of the Christian Gospel – God forgives sinners and, more than that, He accounts them as righteous in His own eyes!

But let us be certain of one thing: justification is not God putting men right, or making men right. It is God acting as if a man (or a woman) already is right! It's a word that comes from the legal world. If a man appears before a judge, and that man is proved to be innocent of the crime with which he had been charged, then to treat him as innocent is to acquit him – and he is thus justified. But the amazing; the astounding; thing about the justification of which Paul here speaks is that when man appears before Almighty God he is not innocent; he is anything but innocent; he is utterly and undeniably guilty! And yet Almighty God, the Judge of all the earth, in His amazing and infinite mercy, treats him, reckons him, accounts him, as if he were innocent. He treats me, not as I most certainly deserve, but 'just as if I'd' never sinned at all.

And, as we will discover in the next chapter, it is not the same as sanctification. Sanctification is the process by which God makes the believer – the disciple of Jesus – more and more like the Saviour. It's a process that continues until physical death transports the believer into the nearer Presence of the Lord.

Justification is a single act. When a sinner places his/her trust in the Lord Jesus Christ – having confessed their sinfulness, repented, and sought His forgiveness, Almighty God immediately declares that person righteous, and that declaration will never be repealed. It is a declaration made in heaven, and made for eternity.

And this leads us on to the second guideline to our answer Having discovered something of the meaning of justification – what it is – we must look at the motive for justification.

And here, we'll try to work out the 'Why?' of justification. Just why is God willing to – indeed, why does He desire to – treat us as if we were innocent?   According to Martin Luther, in his Commentary on Paul's Letter to the Romans, "This is the chief point and central place of the epistle and of the whole Bible." (*in loc*).

The answer is that we are justified "by grace" – that grace at which we looked in an earlier chapter. It is God's love (see chap. 15) that causes Him to act in this way; that love that only He can show; that *agape* of which one expositor says, "It should never be forgotten that *agape* is a word born within the bosom of revealed religion; it occurs in the Septuagint [*which is the Greek translation of the O.T.*], but there is no example of its use in any heathen writer whatever." (R.C.Trench)

"No example of its use in any heathen writer whatever." It is the love that is, pre-eminently, of God; the love that is only attained by us as the process of sanctification is completed. Of course, that process can never be completed in this life; while we inhabit these mortal bodies; while we are still tainted with sin. In other words, I would maintain that we are incapable of giving that level of love until the Day when, by His grace, those who are His see the Saviour face-to-face, and not as through a darkened glass; that Day when we will know, even as we are known; that Day when we will be enabled to offer to Him that love that He, in His mercy and grace, offers to us. And that's the wonder of it all – that although we are unable to truly give that love, that *agape*, now; we may experience it. We are justified – accounted righteous – because God loves us!

And this is so very necessary for each one of us! For, as we read in the 23rd verse of that 3rd chapter of Paul's letter to the church in Rome,

> *"All have sinned ..."*

Not just some, but all! What a blow to the ego this can be for some of us who, like the Pharisee in Jesus' story judge ourselves by other men!

> "God, I thank Thee that I am not like other men, extortioners, unjust, adulterers, or even like this tax collector. I fast twice a week, I give tithes of all that I get." (Lk.18:11[(b)]– 12).

But it was not this man, said Jesus, who

> "... returned home justified before God." (v.14);

it was, by implication, the tax collector, who recognised, and confessed before God, his sinful state!

> "Let him who is without sin cast the first stone"

said Jesus to a group of men, on another occasion. (John 8:7). And not one of those involved was able to claim to be in that state!

> "All have sinned ..."

– and in the depth of our hearts, each one of us knows the truth of that statement with regard to ourselves.

> "All have sinned ..."

– and, therefore, all need to be justified. And Almighty God justifies because of His love for us; and also, as Paul further points out, because this shows that

> "He [God] *Himself is just*" (v.26)

The meaning of justification – God treating me "just-as-if-I'd" never sinned;

The motive for justification – God's infinite love towards mankind; and, finally and, from a practical point of view, most importantly of all, we consider the manner of justification.

The meaning of justification told us what it is; the motive for justification told us why it is. But, although, like the salvation to which it is so closely related, it is freely available to all who will accept it, justification is not a mere hand-out. It is the end-result of a positive course of action. And so, the manner of justification tells us 'how' it is. How can I be justified? This was Job's question. How can I attain this place where God, in His love, treats me as if I had never sinned – not even once!?

Paul, in ch.4 of his letter to the young church in Rome, uses Abraham as an illustration, and reminds his readers, now as well as then, that

"Abraham put his faith in God, and that faith was counted to him as righteousness." (4:3; Gen.15:6).

It was not Abraham's works that made him right in the sight of God; even 'though, if any men were to fit to be justified by works, he was surely one of them! So all of our good deeds aren't enough to justify us. And Paul goes on to say that Abraham was accounted righteous before he was circumcised. That is to say that all of our religious ceremonies, no matter how sincere we may be in them, cannot, of themselves, justify us. And Abraham was accounted as righteous; he was justified; before the giving of the Law. Therefore, says Paul, even strict observance of the Law cannot justify.

Works cannot justify; religious ceremonies cannot justify; keeping the Law cannot justify. And so, we find that the only means of justification is faith – for Abraham, it was faith in El Shaddai, Almighty God; for you and for me, it is faith in the supreme revelation of that same God, even the Son, the Lord Jesus, the Christ. Faith is only as good as its object. I may have faith in a certain chair; I demonstrate my faith by sitting on that chair; but if the chair is broken, I fall to the ground. The object of my faith was not worthy of it! But the disciple of Jesus trusts in, has faith in, that same Jesus. Some may profess a sort of general belief in the existence of a supernatural being to whom they refer with the word 'God'. But that is not what saves us; that is not the way to justification. It is only a personal, individual, faith in Jesus, the Christ, that saves and justifies the lost sinner. Don't forget that even the devils believe in God, and tremble – but this does not bring them salvation! (James 2:19).

God justifies him

> *"who has faith in Jesus."* (v.26)

"And ... how much more satisfying it is", writes F.F.Bruce, "to know oneself 'justified freely by His grace', than to hope to be justified by the deeds of the law. In the latter case," he continues, "I can never really be satisfied that I have 'made the grade', that my behaviour has been sufficiently meritorious to win the divine approval. Even if I do the best I can (and the trouble is that I don't always do even that), how can I be certain that my best comes within measurable distance of God's requirement? I may hope, but I can never be sure. But if God, in sheer grace, assures me of His acceptance in advance, and I gladly embrace His assurance, then I can go on to do His will without always worrying about whether I am doing it adequately, or not. In fact," he concludes, "to the end of my life I shall be [*no more than*] an 'unprofitable servant', but I know Whom I have believed:
'He owns me for His child; I can no longer fear.'" (*Romans*; The Tyndale Press, London, 1969; p.103).

And let us rejoice that this justification is available to all people – regardless of gender, or age, or nationality, or height, or weight, or shape, or intellectual ability, or skin colour, or anything else.

> *"All have sinned..."*

we noted earlier. But because all have sinned; because each one of us is guilty in the sight of the Holy and sinless God; He offers salvation, and the opportunity to be justified, also to all.

And, like everything else, it is a work of His grace. Augustus Toplady knew that when he wrote the lovely hymn "Rock of Ages, cleft for me". Think on these words from that song:

"Not the labours of my hands can fulfil Thy law's demands;
Could my zeal no respite know, could my tears for ever flow,
All for sin could not atone:
Thou must save, and Thou alone!" (Augustus Montague Toplady).

It is all of grace. That's what Paul says:

> "*Being justified freely, by His grace; through the redemption that is in Christ Jesus:*" (v.24).

And note that word "freely". My justification, as my salvation, is free to me. There was a cost – a great cost – but I do not pay it, for Jesus already has. The story is told of a minister who was trying to explain this free salvation and justification to a coal-miner, but the man seemed unable to grasp the concept. "If it's that good, I have to pay for it." he argued. Suddenly, the minister was inspired to ask him "How did you get down the mine today, and back up?" "That was no problem", replied the miner, "I stepped into the cage and the big wheel let me down, and pulled me back up." "Was that not too easy?" enquired the minister. "Of course not," laughed the man, "and it must have cost the company a pretty penny to have all of that machinery installed." He suddenly realised what the preacher had been saying to him. "It doesn't cost me anything to be saved; but it cost God the life of His only-begotten Son."

Salvation, and its associated justification, are both free – the cost comes as we seek to serve our new Master and Lord and discover that He wants us to lay everything on the altar. But it's the altar of His love, and He always repays our sacrifices, as they become a sweet savour unto Him.

"*Can a man be justified before God?*"

asked Job. "Yes", we may reply, "he can. Not by anything that he can say, or do; not because of any standard that he can attain; but by accepting, by faith, what has been done, by Father God, in and through the Christ, for him"

The meaning of justification – God treating me, not as I deserve, but 'just-as-if-I'd' never sinned;

The motive for justification – God's eternal love towards a sinful mankind;

The manner of justification – A living faith, in the living Christ.

God grant that all who read these pages might have the personal assurance of justification "

> *... by the free gift of God's grace ... through Christ Jesus, Who sets [us] free."* (v.24, GNB).

Chapter 12

HOLINESS

"Take time to be holy, speak oft with thy Lord;
Abide in Him always, and feed on His Word."
(W.D.Longstaff, 1822-94)

Holiness! I wonder what that word means to you! The popular idea is one of perfection. If I claim to be holy, then I am claiming to be perfect in every respect. Sadly, those who know me – and especially those who know me best – would be all too aware of how false such a claim would be!

So what is it; why should I want it; and how do I get it?

The Bible speaks of holiness 38 times according to my computerised concordance. But when I typed in the associated adjective, "holy", I simply wasn't able to count the references that came up! The conclusion drawn from that brief exercise was that holiness is something that is important to the Lord. Indeed, contrary to what many of the songs that we sing today say; contrary to what is often preached, today; contrary to what many of the books on the shelves of Christian bookshops would have us believe; the emphasis in God's Word is not on the love of God – important 'though that is – but on the holiness of God. We could press that a little further, and say that even the love of God is a holy love!

Holiness, in the Bible, isn't a negative thing to do with no more than the absence of defilement. It is something that is positive, and active. The word that is used in the Hebrew Scriptures – our Old Testament – and that we translate as "holy" is the word *q'dosh*. This was the cry of the seraphim in Isaiah's great vision, recorded in chap 6 of his prophetic book –

> "*q'dosh, q'dosh, q'dosh, YHWH Sabaoth*" = "*Holy, holy, holy, is the* LORD *of Hosts.*"

Holy is a word that means "that which is set apart; different". So, to the Children of Israel, Shabbat – the 7th day – was holy, because YHWH had set it aside as a day of rest for His chosen people; the priests were holy, because they were set apart to minister to YHWH; the furnishings of the Tabernacle – later the Temple – were holy, because they were dedicated to be used in the worship of YHWH, the Holy One. And so we could go on to mention the garments that the priests wore; the tithes that the people brought the very camp of the Children of Israel. Each one holy, because it was separated from common use, and dedicated to the worship of God.

Our English-language word "holy" comes from the Old English 'halig', meaning to be whole, or healthy. And what good health is to the body, holiness is to the spirit – the inner person.

God, Himself, is – as we've already noted – holy. And He revealed His holiness to His people by giving them a holy law that should have ensured that they would be different to the people who lived around them; by dwelling in the Shekinah Glory in the Holy of holies (most holy place) in the Tabernacle/Temple. Indeed, the very structure of the Tabernacle declared the holiness of YHWH the Holy One of Israel. The great wall/fence of linen (Ex 27:9 around the whole Court of the Sanctuary that separated it from the rest of the camp; the brass laver where the priests washed; the great brass altar where the blood of the sacrifice was shed; the veil/curtain that separated the most holy place from everything else, and into which only the High Priest could go – and that, only once a year after special ceremonies and sacrifices; all of these spoke clearly of the 'otherness', the 'holiness' of Almighty God.

God's holiness is expressed in His works.

> *"The Lord is righteous in all His ways, and holy in all His works"* (Ps. 145:17).

Nothing but that which is excellent can proceed from Him. Holiness is the rule of all His actions. At the beginning He pronounced all that He made *"very good"* (Gen. 1:31), which He could not have done had there been anything imperfect or unholy in them. Man was made *"upright"* (Eccl. 7:29), in the image and likeness of his Creator. The angels that fell were created holy, but we are told that they

> *"did not stay within the limits of authority God gave them"* (Jude 6).

Even of the satan it is written,

> *"You were blameless in all you did from the day you were created until the day evil was found in you."* (Ezek. 28:15).

God's holiness is manifested in His law. That law forbids sin in **all** of its variations: in its most refined as well as its worst forms, the intent of the mind as well as the action/inaction of the body, the secret desire as well as the actual deed. So we read,

> *"The law is holy, and the commandment is holy, and just, and good"* (Rom. 7:12).

And because God is holy He **hates all sin**. He loves everything which is in line with His law; but He loathes everything which is contrary to it. His Word plainly declares,

> *"violent people ... are an abomination to the Lord"* (Prov. 3:32).

And again,

> *"YHWH detests the thoughts of the wicked"* (Prov. 15:26).

It follows, therefore, that He must necessarily punish sin. Praise God, He has often forgiven sinners, but He never forgives sin; and the sinner is only forgiven on the ground of Another having borne his punishment for, as the bronze altar reminded the early Israelites,

> *"without shedding of blood is no remission"* (Heb. 9:22).

God's holiness is manifested at the Cross. Wondrously, and yet most solemnly, does the Atonement (see ch.6) display God's infinite holiness and abhorrence of sin. How hateful must sin be to God for Him to punish it to its utmost desserts when it was imputed to His Son as He took the sin of mankind upon His own Body on the Cross of Calvary. Indeed, the Lord Jesus did not 'merely' take my sin – and yours – upon Himself; He did not 'merely' pay the penalty that you and I deserved to pay. He did all of that, but what happened at Calvary was much, much, costlier for the spotless Lamb of God. Paul, writing to the believers in Corinth shares with them this amazing; this astounding; this almost unbelievable fact –

> *"For our sake He* [Father God] *made Him* [the Lord Jesus] ***to be sin*** *Who knew no sin, so that in Him we might become the righteousness of God."* (II Cor. 5:21; *emphasis added*).

Do you understand what the apostle is saying? He is saying that Jesus actually 'became sin' for us. He is saying that Jesus became, for a brief moment of human time, all of the ugliness; the vileness; the awfulness; that is sin. Little wonder that the Father turned His eyes away from the Son, causing Him to cry out in despair

> *"My God, My God, why have You forsaken me?"* (Matt.27:46; Mark 15:34).

Could this be what the prophet Isaiah saw as he was allowed to peer into the mists of future time and see that One hanging on a cross?

> *"There was nothing beautiful or majestic about His appearance, nothing to attract us to Him."* (Isa 53:2; NLT).

"Not all the vials of judgment that have or shall be poured out upon the wicked world, nor the flaming furnace of a sinner's conscience, nor the irreversible sentence pronounced against the rebellious demons, nor the groans of the damned creatures, give such a demonstration of God's hatred of sin, as the wrath of God let loose upon His Son. Never did Divine holiness appear more beautiful and lovely than at the time our Saviour's countenance was most marred in the midst of His dying groans. This He Himself acknowledges in Ps. 22:1. When God had turned His smiling face from Him, and thrust His sharp knife into His heart, forcing that terrible cry from Him, "My God, My God, why hast Thou forsaken Me?" He adores this perfection—"Thou art holy," v.3" (Stephen Charnock – 17th century English Presbyterian clergyman).

Holiness – an attribute of Almighty God that speaks of His otherness; His differentness; His separation from all that is corrupt, and shameful, and abhorrent.

But why should I want it?

The simplest answer to that question is "Because He says so"!

Time and time again, we read words such as these:

> *"For I am YHWH your God; consecrate yourselves therefore, and **be holy**, for I am holy."* (Lev 11:44 – *emphasis added*).

God's purpose for Israel was that the nation be

> *"... a kingdom of priests, my **holy** nation."* (Ex 19:6).

The oft-neglected book of Leviticus shows that the Jewish people were distinguished by their diet; their treatment of new-born infants – and their mothers; their treatment of the dead; their handling of those who were diseased; personal cleanliness; and marriage. And while there were definite advantages in terms of e.g. hygiene in the regulations that they were given, the bottom line was that they were constant reminders that God's people couldn't live in just any way they pleased.

We read from Peter's first letter to the early Christian Church –

> *"... you are a chosen people. You are a kingdom of priests, **God's holy nation**, His very own possession. This is so that you can show others the goodness of God, for He called you out of the darkness into His wonderful light."* (I Peter 2:9; *emphasis added*).

God's church is supposed to be *"a holy nation"* in this present evil world. And anyone who would dispute that evil, cannot possibly be reading a newspaper, or listening to a news bulletin. A little girl tortured and killed by her own mother and the mother's boyfriend; another mother guilty of colluding in the systematic sexual abuse of her daughter by a ring of paedophiles; a 17 year-old charged with the murder of an 18 year-old – and that's only part of one day's news!

Those who have not been born again have no real conception of God's holiness, let alone a desire to believe in it. Many, therefore, make the mistake of assuming that God's character is one-sided, that His great mercy will override everything else, and that there is no need for any alarm.

> *"... you thought that I was one like yourself."* (Ps. 50:21)

is God's charge against them. They think only of a "god" patterned after their own evil hearts. But the holiness ascribed to the Divine nature and character in the Scriptures clearly demonstrates their superhuman origin. The character attributed to the "gods" of the ancients and of modern non-Christians is the very reverse of that immaculate purity which belongs to the true God. An indescribably holy God, who has the utmost abhorrence of all sin, was never invented by any of Adam's fallen descendants! The fact is that nothing makes the terrible depravity of man's heart and his enmity against the living God more obvious than to have set before him One who is infinitely and unchangeably holy. Man's own idea of **sin** is, to all intent, limited to what the world calls "crime." Anything short of that man excuses as "defects," "mistakes," "infirmities," etc. And even where sin is owned at all, excuses and justifications are made for it.

The "god" which even the vast majority of professing Christians "love" is looked upon very much like an indulgent old man, who himself has no appetite for sin, but who leniently, and conveniently, winks at the "indiscretions" of mankind. But God's Word says,

> *"You hate **all** who do evil"* (Ps. 5:5).

And again,

> *"God is a judge who is perfectly fair. He is angry with the wicked every day."* (Ps. 7:11).

But men refuse to believe in *this* God, and are angered when His hatred of sin is clearly brought to their attention.

It is because God is holy that we should desire to be like Him. His command, we read, is,

> "*You must be holy, **because I am holy**"* (I Pet. 1:16, *emphasis added*).

We are not commanded to be omnipotent or omniscient as He is, but we are to be holy and, writes Peter,

> "*... you must be holy in everything you do, just as God — who chose you to be his children — is holy."* (I Peter 1:15).

"This is the prime way of honouring God. We do not so glorify God by elevated admirations, or eloquent expressions, or pompous services of Him, as when we aspire to a conversing with Him with unstained spirits, and live to Him in living *like* Him" (Stephen Charnock).

What is holiness? An attribute of Almighty God that speaks of his otherness; His differentness; His separation from all that is corrupt and shameful, and abhorrent.

Why should I want it? Because He has commanded that I should be holy, even as He is holy; and because I should want to be conformed to the image of the Son. Only one important question remains! And that is "How do I get it?"

Well, as God alone is the Source and Fount of holiness, we must seek holiness from Him. Let our daily prayer be that He may

> "*... make* (us) *holy in every way, and (that our) whole spirit and soul and body be kept blameless until that day when our Lord Jesus Christ comes again."* (I Thess. 5:23).

In the New Testament, the word that is used is the word '*hagios*'. Indeed, that is the word that is used to translate the Hebrew *q'dosh* in the Greek version of the Old Testament – the Septuagint.

Christ's people are regularly called "saints" or holy persons, and holiness in the high ethical and spiritual meaning of the word is used to denote the appropriate quality of their life and conduct. No doubt, as applied to believers, "saints" conveys in the first place the notion of a separation from the world and a consecration to God. Just as Israel under the old covenant was a chosen race, so the Christian church in succeeding to Israel's privileges becomes a holy nation, and the Christian individual, as one of the elect people, becomes a holy man or woman (Col. 3:12). In Paul's usage all baptised believers are "saints," however far they may still be from the saintly character (compare I Cor. 1:2,14 with 5:1 ff). But though the use of the name does not imply high ethical character as a realized fact, it always assumes it as an ideal and an obligation. It is taken for granted that the Holy Spirit has taken up His abode in the heart of every regenerate person, and that a work of positive sanctification is going on there. The New Testament leaves no room for the thought of a holiness divorced from those moral qualities which the holy God demands of those whom He has called to be His people.

And that means that, if I am to be holy, I must have come to the Lord Jesus Christ, in humility and faith; confessing my sinfulness/unholiness; accepting His sacrificial death in my place; repenting/turning away from my sinfulness; and accepting the new life of holiness that He offers.

Have you ever done that? Or have you made the mistake of seeking to worship a god made in your own image? Come to Him right now; to the Holy One Whose desire is that you and I be holy too. It will be for your eternal good, and to His eternal glory.

Chapter 13

RIGHTEOUSNESS

*"You're my all; You're the best;
You're my joy, my righteousness;
And I love You, Lord."*
(Graham Kendrick)

In his challenging, but highly recommended, book *The Gospel according to Jesus* (Zondervan; 1988, 1994), John F. MacArthur has a chapter entitled: "He receives sinners, but refuses the righteous". With all respect to such an experienced author, and a man who has a deeper grasp of Christian theology than I will ever have, I would suggest that this is a deceptive title. Reading through the chapter does make it much clearer as he writes, concerning the words of Jesus recorded in Matt. 9:13 – *"... I did not come to call the righteous, but sinners ..."* (NKJV) – "Jesus' words were aimed at the self-righteous Pharisees who, like many today, thought they were righteous and without any real spiritual need." (p.68).

It is that little word "self" that makes the difference for, as Paul reminds us, quoting loosely from the Book of Psalms,

"None is righteous, no, not one;" (Rom 3:10).

So, it follows, that there would be no-one for Jesus to refuse, in terms of the chapter title. Dr MacArthur does further clarify the situation as he continues: "God receives sinners. The flip side of that is that He refuses "the righteous". **Not that there are any truly righteous people, of course** (Rom.3:10). But those who think they are good enough – those who do not understand the seriousness of sin – cannot respond to the Gospel." (p.72; *emphasis added*).

The first thing, then, that we may note about righteousness, is that it is not a quality of natural, fallen, mankind. Left to my own devices, I can never be righteous. I may fool myself that I am – but in the laser-like gaze of the all-holy God, all of my self-deception is stripped away, and I am forced to confess that I am anything but righteous.

Part of the clue to the meaning of righteous(ness) is in the first five letters of the word. Righteousness has to do with being – being right in the sight of that all-holy God. It is, therefore, closely related to justification, at which we looked in chapter 11. As a heading to that chapter, I quoted some words of the systematic theologian, Louis Berkhof, who defines justification as "... a judicial act of God, in which He declares, on the basis of the righteousness of Jesus Christ, that all the claims of the law are satisfied with respect to the sinner." So, we discovered, justification is God treating me "just as if I'd" never sinned. Righteousness, we might say, is God providing the means – "... the righteousness of Jesus ..." – by which He might treat me in such a gracious way. I have no righteousness that I may claim for myself – through the Jewish prophet, Isaiah, the Lord makes this situation abundantly clear.

> "*We have all become like one who is unclean, and all our righteous deeds are like a polluted garment.*" (or "*filthy*

rags" as the A.V. so much more graphically puts it!). (Isa 64:6).

But Father God, in the Persona of Jesus, the Son, provides the very righteousness of which I am by nature incapable. To use the language of a former generation, "I am covered with His (Jesus') righteousness."

The Life Application Bible Commentary on Ephesians (Tyndale House) offers some helpful insight: "Righteousness ... ... gives the evidence that we have been made right with God and that this righteousness has been given us by the Holy Spirit. Believers have been made righteous through the blood of Christ. The believers then want to live in uprightness and integrity, desiring to please the One who saved them. Yet that won't be easy. Satan is ready for battle at every turn, willing to hit us unfairly from behind if given the chance" (p. 132).

So how may the righteousness of Christ be displayed in the lives of His disciples? May I suggest that it may be seen, first of all, by an inner integrity?

The Pharisees of Jesus' time were men who held the Torah, the Law of Moses (really the Law of YHWH as delivered to Moses), in the highest regard. Matthew 23 is an interesting discourse by the Lord.

> *"Then said Jesus to the crowds and to His disciples, 'The scribes and the Pharisees sit on Moses' seat; so practice and observe whatever they tell you, but not what they do; for they preach, but do not practice.'"* (vs 1-3).

What is Jesus saying here? Well, Moses was seen as having been the great legislator for the Jewish people, and the task of expounding and explaining that law was given to the scribes and the Pharisees. Traditionally, they sat as they taught and rose when they read from the Torah. So, what Jesus is saying is that they had the authority to teach the sacred Law. But note what He goes on to say – that His disciples are to do what the scribes and the Pharisees teach, but not copy what they do!

The problem with the Pharisees (and the scribes?) was that their religion was based on outward actions and appearance – but their hearts were not right before Almighty God. Were his former fellow-Pharisees also in the mind of the apostle Paul when he wrote to Timothy about those who, within the professing church, were

> "... holding the form of religion but denying the power of it." (II Tim.3:5)?

Disciples of Jesus are not to be like that.

Indeed, Jesus said,

> "... I tell you, unless your righteousness exceeds that of the scribes and Pharisees, you will never enter the kingdom of heaven." (Matt.5:20)

– words that would have left a first-century Jew feeling helpless unable to achieve even that standard of ethical living displayed by the Pharisees! Our imputed (that just means received from another – in this case, the Lord Jesus) righteousness is to be displayed by our innermost being – not just a show that we put on for the benefit of others. My most sincere desire must be to do the right thing at all times, as a good witness to my Lord and Saviour. I will fail, of course. Sadly, in this life I shall never attain sinless perfection. But it must be my constant goal; the destination towards which constantly, and consistently, travel. That, as we shall discover in the next chapter, is the process of sanctification.

In his book *The Scandal of the Evangelical Conscience,* Ronald J Sider refers to those well-known words of the risen and exalted Jesus to the church in Laodicea:

> *"Behold, I stand at the door and knock; if any one hears My voice and opens the door, I will come in to him and eat with him, and he with Me."* (Rev. 3:20).

Recognising that those words were written, not to the unsaved, but to those who claimed to have been saved, he writes, with piercing accuracy, "Evangelicals have used the image of Christ knocking at the heart's door as a symbol of our vigorous evangelistic programmes. But in truth, it is we, by our behaviour, who have excluded Him from our hearts and lives. He stands at the doors of *our* hearts, begging us to welcome His total Lordship.

"Weeping and repentance are the only faithful responses to the sweeping, scandalous disobedience in the evangelical world today. We have defied the Lord we claim to worship. We have disgraced His holy Name by our unholy lives. Yes, we believe He is the Saviour. We are Christians, not pagans. But our beliefs are not strong enough to produce righteous lifestyles. We want Jesus and mammon. Unless we repent, our Lord intends to spit us out." (pps. 122-123).

But if I display the righteousness of Christ by my inner integrity, I must also display it by my social involvement. This is one of the discoveries that I have made in my own spiritual pilgrimage. There is a social aspect to the outworking of the Gospel message.

Some of the commentaries on the letter of James have 'titles' such as "Belief that behaves"; "What faith should do"; or "The 24/7 Christian". This is because the true Christian life is as much about what actions I take, as about my doctrine! The Gospel of Jesus Christ is for the whole person, not just the 'soul person'.

> *"What does it profit, my brethren, if a man says he has faith but has not works? Can his faith save him? If a brother or sister is ill-clad and in lack of daily food, and one of you says to them, "Go in peace, be warmed and filled," without giving them the things needed for the body, what does it profit? So faith by itself, if it has no works, is dead. But someone will say, "You have faith and I have works." Show me your faith apart from your works, and I by my works will show you my faith. You believe that God is one; you do well. Even the demons believe - and shudder."* (James 2:14-19).

It is, surely, no accident that so many of the great social reformers of history have been followers of the Nazarene. Were they not following the teaching of the parable of the Good Samaritan? Elizabeth Fry campaigned for prison reform; William Wilberforce brought about the abolition of the slave-trade; men like the Earl of Shaftesbury, and Dr Thomas Barnardo, took up the cause of working, and abandoned, children; William and Catherine Booth were instrumental in the bringing about of meaningful social work among the poor of London, and beyond. The list could be expanded almost indefinitely for, in every age, there have been, and continue to be, those whose Christian faith was, and is, a public affair with social implications. Their righteousness – their right living before God – was, and is, manifest in their social involvement.

One of the blights of evangelical Christianity in the latter part of the 20th century was the emphasis on personal faith, and 'private' religion. The Christian faith, many claimed, does not speak to social issues. I recall, in a fellowship to which I once belonged, being asked if, in the run-up to a General Election, I would speak for a few minutes to the mid-week meeting on the subject of the believer and the vote. It was one who had been a member of similar fellowships for much longer than I, who informed me that even a few years earlier, having someone speak on such a topic, in such a place, would have been unthinkable!

Yet when we read some of the pronouncements of Jesus, as recorded for us by the Gospel writers, we discover that He preached a strong socio-political message. He was definitely not the a-political being that many prefer to think. This, I suspect, is because the very concept of politics, in this early part of the 21st century, has come to have extremely negative connotations. We see wheeling and dealing; scheming and spinning; corruption and compromise. We see politicians who appear to be more interested in feathering their own nests, than in making wise and just laws for the benefit of a whole society; fighting for power; jockeying for position. We hear slandering and mud-slinging; half-truths and party propaganda; insincerity and duplicity. We long for men and women of honesty and integrity to occupy the corridors of secular power.

Now there are, of course, some truly honourable exceptions. But the picture of the political world that most of us have is negative in the extreme. We no longer trust our political representatives – who seem to do anything other than represent us!

In that context, it is easy to understand why some do not wish to see Jesus tainted by any reference to politics in the Gospel record. Yet He made many statements that, when understood in the context of 1st century Palestine, were politically charged.

Take, for example, His first – and, perhaps, only – 'formal' sermon, preached in the synagogue in Nazareth, the town in which he had been raised (Luke 4:16ff). He began, we might say, by announcing His text. It was taken from the book (or, for Him at that time, scroll) of the prophet Isaiah, at the place that we now know as 61:1-2.

> *"The Spirit of the Lord is upon me, because He has anointed me to preach good news to the poor. He has sent me to proclaim release to the captives and recovering of sight to the blind, to set at liberty those who are oppressed, to proclaim the acceptable year of the Lord."*

Those words were, originally, spoken to the Jewish exiles in Babylon, and were a promise from YHWH that they would be granted their freedom, and would be permitted to return to the land of their fathers. The gathered congregation waited to hear what He would say. His first words –

> *"Today this scripture has been fulfilled in your hearing."*
> (Luke 4:21)

– were welcomed. But then He continued, and what He now said they found disturbing. He told them that He recognised that they were expecting Him to perform the kind of miracles that they had of Him performing in Capernaum. But their expectations were not going to be met! He pointed out that the great Jewish prophets, Elijah and Elisha, were sent to heal non-Israelites! That was a politically-charged statement – and led to their trying to hurl Him from the brow of the hill on which Nazareth was built.

So what was the political aspect of His message? Well, the last words of the quotation refer to the proclamation of

> *"... the acceptable year of the Lord."*

In Leviticus 25, the Children of Israel were instructed to observe two special year-long celebrations. The first of these was the sabbatical year (every seventh), when the land was to be allowed complete rest – no sowing; no reaping. The other was the Year of Jubilee. This was to take place every fifty years (i.e. after seven sabbatical years) and, during that year, as well as the restrictions on sowing and reaping, the Children of Israel were to free slaves, forgive debts, and restore land to its original owners!

Can you imagine what an effect all of that would have on a society? The intention was that the disadvantaged would be granted a new beginning. It was a means of ensuring that the rich didn't get any richer, and that the poor didn't get any poorer. Even as I type, the world is still in a state of financial and economic difficulty – and most of it seems to have stemmed from the greed of many of the rich, and the laziness of many of the poor. But here we have the Divine idea of economic and social justice – and it's a political statement of mind-boggling dimensions.

This socio-political aspect of the Gospel, and of our righteousness in Christ, has to do with His Lordship. According to Paul, Jesus is

> "... *the image of the invisible God, the first-born of all creation; for in Him all things were created, in heaven and on earth, visible and invisible, whether thrones or dominions or principalities or authorities - all things were created through Him and for Him. He is before all things, and in Him all things hold together. He is the head of the body, the church; He is the beginning, the first-born from the dead, that in everything He might be pre-eminent. For in Him all the fulness of God was pleased to dwell, and through Him to reconcile to Himself all things, whether on earth or in heaven, making peace by the blood of His cross."* (Col. 1:15-20).

"He is", as the preachers of an earlier generation would often say, "... Lord **of** all; or He is not Lord **at** all!" And that "all" doesn't exclude social and political issues, and the social and political well-being of my fellow human being.

It was interesting to note, as I researched for this chapter (one of those that wasn't included in that original series of sermons!), the number of scholarly books that have been written since the end of the twentieth century, on the topic of the social Gospel – that is not an 'alternative' to the Good News of salvation by faith in the Lord Jesus, but is the outworking of that faith.

> "... *by grace you have been saved through faith; and this is not your own doing, it is the gift of God - not because of works, lest any man should boast. For we are His workmanship, created in Christ Jesus **for good works, which God prepared beforehand, that we should walk in them.***" (Eph.2:8-10; *emphasis added*).

> "*Let your light so shine before men, **that they may see your good works** and give glory to your Father Who is in heaven.*" (Matt.5:16; *emphasis added*).

> "*Let us hold fast the confession of our hope without wavering, for He who promised is faithful; and let us consider how to stir up one another to love **and good works**,*" (Heb.10:23-24; *emphasis added*).

Righteousness – displayed by my inner integrity, and my social involvement; and both driven by the divine imperative. My concern for the persecuted church; my, albeit limited, political activism; my involvement with those who make no claim to be of the Kingdom of God; are all motivated by commands such as that given through the writer of the Letter to Hebrew disciples of Jesus:

> "*Do not neglect to do good and to share what you have, for such sacrifices are pleasing to God.*" (Heb 13:16).

Paul, too, exhorts his readers:

"And let us not grow weary in well-doing, for in due season we shall reap, if we do not lose heart. So then, as we have opportunity, let us do good to all men, and especially [but not solely!] *to those who are of the household of faith."* (Gal.6:9-10).

So, as in everything else, the praise and the glory go to Him – the Author and the Finisher of our faith; our Redeemer and our Righteousness.

Chapter 14

SANCTIFICATION

"May God Himself, the God of peace, sanctify you through and through. May your whole spirit, soul and body be kept blameless at the coming of our Lord Jesus Christ. The one Who calls you is faithful and He will do it." (I Thess. 5:23-24)

More out of curiosity than anything else, I lifted down my dictionary to check on the meaning of the word at which we look in this chapter – the word 'sanctification'. And, under the verb from which the noun is derived, the word 'sanctify', I read: "to make, declare, regard as, or show to be, sacred or holy; to set apart for sacred use; to free from sin or evil; to consecrate; to invest with a sacred character; to make efficient as the means of holiness." (Chambers Twentieth Century Dictionary).

In the letter to the early Hebrew believers, and in what we refer to as the 12th verse of the 13th chapter, we read that

"Jesus ... suffered, outside the gate, in order to sanctify the people through His own blood."

So, if we put all of this information together, we discover that Jesus died on the cross in order that those who trust in Him for salvation might be declared, regarded as, shown to be sacred or holy; that they might be set apart for sacred use; freed from sin or evil;

consecrated; invested with a sacred character; made efficient as the means of holiness. Or, in other, simpler, words: Jesus died, He shed His blood, in order that those who trust in Him might become like Him. And this is what sanctification is all about – becoming like Jesus; growing in Him; becoming holy, even as He is holy.

As we look at this word, and seek to get to know it better, I want to point out three things about it; three things that show it to be what it is – not an instant achievement, but a gradual, and often painful, process bringing about changes so that different stages, or even grades, may be distinguished in the resulting holiness. As one preacher/theologian writes: "We must distinguish between cleansing and holiness. You cannot be holy without being cleansed; but you can be cleansed without being holy. The Book of Leviticus is divided into two parts: the first part is about cleansing, and the second is about holiness. Cleansing is by an act; holiness never is. There can be no holiness until there is cleansing. Cleansing is never progressive; holiness always is – and they are intimately related." (Graham Scroggie). Sanctification is the name given to that process; that progression towards holiness.

Like every process, sanctification must have a beginning. And we find that it is commenced at conversion.

It begins as soon as I give control of my life to Jesus; as soon as I open my heart's door to Him; as soon as I acknowledge my own sinfulness, and my total inability to deal with it; and accept His free offer of full salvation. It is the immediate follow-up to the justification at which we looked in an earlier chapter – God's treating me 'just-as-if-I'd' never sinned does, in fact, declare me to be holy; set apart for His use; consecrated. He declares me to be different; to have become one of His children, by adoption into His family; truly able to call Him 'Father'. But this is only the beginning of the process.

So we see that sanctification is for real Christians. If we were to ask the question "Who are sanctified?", the answer would be "Believing people". If I have truly trusted in Jesus; if I have yielded my life, fully and unreservedly, to Him; then I am being sanctified. If I have not made that move of commitment, then I am not! For sanctification begins at conversion. Just as physical growth begins, in one sense, at birth; so spiritual growth – which is what sanctification is – begins at rebirth. I have a long way to go; I will make many mistakes; I will fall down again and again. But I will have started!

But beginnings are usually followed by middles and endings. And so we find that sanctification has a second stage. It is commenced at conversion, and it is continued in Christian living.

There are some, of course, who would claim that they have already attained fully sanctified living – sinless perfection! I once met a member of 'ISKCON' (the International Society for Krishna Consciousness; commonly referred to as Hari Krishna, because of their chant using that phrase) who made such a claim. I don't want to go into a lesson on Hinduism, and reincarnation, but I have sometimes wondered if he was merely fed up with his alleged cycle of birth, life, death, and rebirth, and was desperately keen to attain nirvana!

However, as the New Bible Dictionary points out, such high claims "… usually minimise both the description of sin and the standard of moral living required. Sin", it goes on, "is defined [by such] as 'the voluntary transgression of a known law' (Wesley) rather than as 'any want of conformity unto, or transgression of, the law of God' (Westminster Shorter Catechism), the latter being a definition that covers our sinful state, and sins of omission as well as sins openly and deliberately committed." (*in loc*).

And such claims to sinless perfection – made also by some who claim to be disciples of Jesus – disregard the very Word of God. The question of Solomon is still pertinent:

> *"Who can say 'I have made my heart clean, I am pure from my sin'?"* (Prov.20:9).

Moreover, John says:

> *"If we say that we have no sin, we deceive ourselves, and the truth is not in us."* (I John 1:8)

and, even more seriously:

> *"If we say we have not sinned, we make Him [God] a liar and His Word is not in us".* (I John 1:10).

And, of course, it is the experience of every believer that sin becomes more of a reality after conversion than it ever was before. And this is only to be expected! If I am not aware that something is wrong, then I may do it with a clear conscience; if I am not aware that something else ought to be done, then I don't care about not having done it! Ignorance really can be (at least temporarily) bliss!

But as soon as I am made aware of these things then, although I may still do, or fail to do, as the case may be, I now care; I regret; I don't have a clear conscience.

Paul certainly found this to be so. Arguably the greatest Christian who ever lived, he never claimed to have attained a state of sinless perfection! Listen to him, as he writes to the church in Rome:

> *"I don't understand myself at all, for I really want to do what is right, but I don't do it. Instead, I do the very thing I hate. I know perfectly well that what I am doing is wrong, and my bad conscience shows that I agree that the law is*

good. But I can't help myself, because it is sin inside me that makes me do these evil things. I know I am rotten through and through so far as my old sinful nature is concerned. No matter which way I turn, I can't make myself do right. I want to, but I can't. When I want to do good, I don't. And when I try not to do wrong, I do it anyway. But if I am doing what I don't want to do, I am not really the one doing it; the sin within me is doing it. It seems to be a fact of life that when I want to do what is right, I inevitably do what is wrong. I love God's law with all my heart. But there is another law at work within me that is at war with my mind. This law wins the fight and makes me a slave to the sin that is still within me." (7:15-23; NLT).

And each one of us, I suspect, knows the reality of Paul's experience; this tug-of-war that goes on inside us between what we sometimes refer to as our baser, and our finer, instincts. It has been illustrated by the story of the sheep, the pig, and the muddy pool! The pig and the sheep were walking along the path together. They came to a large, muddy, pool that covered almost the full width of the track – leaving just a very narrow track at the edge, that sloped down from the hedgerow. They decided that the track was sufficient for them to make their way around the pool, and the sheep led the way. However, at about the half-way point, the slope was too much for him; he lost his footing, and tumbled into the pool! What a disaster! As quickly as he could, the sheep scrambled out of the pool and started shaking the muddy water from his body.

Meanwhile, the pig was making his way around the pool. At about the same point he, too, lost his footing and tumbled into the pool. His reaction couldn't have been any more different to that of his friend! He wallowed in the mud, finding the whole experience totally enjoyable.

The lesson is that both the disciple of Jesus, and the unconverted person, will fall into sin. The difference is that the person who has invited Jesus to take control of his/her life will not be comfortable in that sin, and will quickly repent and move on in the forgiveness that is offered through the shed blood of Jesus. The unconverted person may be perfectly happy, and continue in that sin.

The difference with Paul, and with any true believer, is that as we continue in our Christian life; as we grow more and more like Jesus; so the good within us wins the battle more often – 'though the very intensity of the battle may well increase as the devil sees us spending more time in prayer and in the study of God's Word; in witnessing to the saving power of Jesus; in helping others for Jesus' sake.

So, while Paul continues in his letter to those Roman believers, with these pessimistic words:

> *"Oh, what a miserable person I am! Who will free me from this life that is dominated by sin?"* (v.24),

he can then burst out with a shout of joy and praise:

> *"Thank God! The answer is in Jesus Christ our Lord."* (v.25; NLT).

Because Jesus died that I might live, and because I have yielded my life to Him, I am indwelt by God the Holy Spirit, and am therefore being sanctified – made more and more like Jesus! Of course, as theologian Louis Berkhof, points out regarding the incompleteness of sanctification in this life, it is not that it is only a part of the believer, like some part that originates at conversion that is affected. Salvation is for the whole man, and no less so is sanctification. Prof. Berkhof writes; "It is the whole, but yet undeveloped new man, that must grow into full stature. A newborn child is, barring exceptions, perfect in parts, but not yet in the degree of development for which it is intended. Just so, the new man is perfect in parts, but remains, in the present life, imperfect in the degree of spiritual development." (Systematic Theology, p.537)

Did you know that? Imperfect as you are; imperfect as I am; if we are believing Christians; if our trust is placed fully, and wholly, in the Lord Jesus; then we already have the potential of perfection within us!

But, of course, we each have our own part to play! I believe that this is why Paul, writing to those early disciples of Jesus in Rome, said:

> *"I appeal to you therefore, brethren, by the mercies of God, to present your bodies as a living sacrifice, holy and acceptable to God, which is your spiritual worship. Do not be conformed to this world but be transformed **by the renewal of your mind**, that you may prove what is the will of God, what is good and acceptable and perfect."* (Rom.12:1-2; *emphasis added*).

You see, it's the mind that is the problem! Like the vast majority of people, I do not involve myself in criminal activities, or even those that are overtly immoral. My speech and my actions tend, in general, to be acceptable to all. But my thoughts!! Now that's a different matter! And, of course, even if I were to be involved in the sort of activity that would have me constantly 'looking over my shoulder', those activities would have started in my mind!

If the mind is being renewed, through the constant work of God the Holy Spirit, then I am being sanctified – made to be more like Jesus.

Thinking on the beginning of the process of sanctification taught us who they are who are being sanctified – those whose trust is placed, fully and wholly, in Jesus. Having thought of the continuing process, we've discovered the 'How?' – through the indwelling power of God the Holy Spirit. But I did say that there's an end to the process. It's commenced at conversion; it begins with the new birth; it continues in Christian living: a never-completed, ongoing process. But, of course, you and I, if we are truly disciples of the Lord Jesus, ought to be able to look back and see an improvement in our lives. Oh, as one matter is settled, the Lord shows me another that must be dealt with; as soon as I find that I am able to stand here, the devil pulls me down there. But, praise God, this process of sanctification is completed in glory.

Someone has said that becoming a Christian doesn't rid one of sin. What happens is that sin is put into the dustbin; the lid is placed on top; we sit on the bin; and we wait until the morning for the lorry to come and the bin to be emptied. But, of course, sin is always active, and sometimes it pushes both me and the lid off, and goes on the rampage again – and I need Jesus' help to put it back in again!

Some of you may have read the book *A Man called Peter*, the biography of Peter Marshall, written by his widow, the late Catherine Marshall (and if you haven't, then I highly recommend it!). Peter Marshall died as a result of a heart attack when he was just 46 years old, and the book ends like this, with Catherine standing on the beach at the little summer cottage on Cape Cod, that held so many precious memories for her. She writes: "Suddenly I remembered something; the last words I had ever spoken to Peter. Was it possible that God had prompted those words, seemingly so casual?

"The scene was etched forever on my mind – Peter, lying on the stretcher where the two orderlies had put him down for a moment while the ambulance waited just outside the front door. Peter had looked up at me, and smiled through his pain, his eyes full of tenderness; and I had leaned close to him and said, 'Darling, I'll see you in the morning'.

"And as I stood, looking out toward that far horizon, , I knew that those words would go singing in my heart down all the years ...

'See you, darling; see you in the morning'." (Peter Davies, London, 1952 pps.284-285).

"See you in the morning". We all know, do we not, what Catherine Marshall had meant when she said those words to her husband as he was taken to hospital. And don't we also know what was in her mind when she remembered them?

For Peter Marshall, the morning had come; the dustbin, with its sin, had been taken away and there, in the nearer presence of his Master, in glory, he was fully sanctified; he was made perfect for all eternity.

That's why death holds no fear for the disciple of Jesus. It was the Indian poet, Rabindranath Tagore (1861-1941), who said that "Death is not extinguishing the light; it is only putting out the lamp because the dawn has come."

Stephen, recognised as the first Christian martyr, is not the only one to have met physical death with courage and faith. As he was being stoned – and these would have been fair-sized boulders, not 'wee chucky-stanes' – we read:

> "But Stephen, full of the Holy Spirit, gazed steadily upward into heaven and saw the glory of God, and he saw Jesus standing in the place of honour at God's right hand. And

he told them, 'Look, I see the heavens opened and the Son of Man standing in the place of honour at God's right hand!' ... And as they stoned him, Stephen prayed, 'Lord Jesus, receive my spirit.' And he fell to his knees, shouting, 'Lord, don't charge them with this sin!' And with that, he died." (Acts 7:55-56, 59-60).

And at that moment, Stephen, too, was fully sanctified.

And so with all who have likewise trusted the Christ. Praise God that, when we finish with this mortal body in what we call 'death', we leave our very sinfulness with it, and become perfect beings; spiritual beings; fit for the nearer presence of the Lord; able to praise and glorify Him as we ought.

"absent from the body, ... present with the Lord"

as Paul reminded the believers in Corinth (II Cor.5:8). Then, and not before, are we fully sanctified.

Sanctification – the process of being made like Jesus:

Who are sanctified? Only true believers – disciples of Jesus - because sanctification begins at conversion.

How are believers sanctified? Through the indwelling power of God the Holy Spirit, as the process continues in Christian living.

When are believers fully sanctified? Only after physical death, as their growing more and more like Jesus is completed in glory; as they become like Him; seeing Him as He is.

To the best of my knowledge, the little printed plaque that is on my study wall is a Brian Ross 'original' (the words, not the sentiment!). It reads, quite simply: "In this life I shall never be sinless but, by God's grace, I may sin less!" And that is sanctification.

There's a challenging hymn by Theodore Monod – a Parisian who wrote the words during a series of Consecration Meetings that were being conducted in Broadlands, Hampshire, England, in 1874. It reads:

Oh, the bitter pain and sorrow;
That a time could ever be
When I let the Saviour's pity
Plead in vain, and proudly answered,
"All of self, and none of Thee!"

Yet He found me; I beheld Him
Bleeding on the accursed tree.
Heard Him pray, "Forgive them, Father!"
And my wistful heart said faintly,
"Some of self, and some of Thee".

Day by day His tender mercy,
Healing, helping, full and free,
Sweet and strong, and ah! so patient,
Brought me lower, while I whispered,
"Less of self, and more of Thee".

Higher than the highest heaven,
Deeper than the deepest sea,
Lord, Thy love at last has conquered:
Grant me, now, my supplication –
"None of self, and all of Thee".

That sums up both the process, and the goal, of sanctification – although none of us fully attain it in this life.

Have you truly believed? Then this work has begun in you and, 'though you will fall, and the devil will try to tell you that you can't be a Christian at all, you can be assured

> *"that He Who began a good work in you, will bring it to completion at the Day of Jesus Christ."* (Phil.1:6).

In this life, I am 'a work in progress'. I shall never be sinless but, by the grace of God, I may sin less!

Chapter 15

PREDESTINATION

"Because of the great chasm between God and man and because of man's sinfulness, God must predestine people into salvation...or none would be saved. Therefore, salvation is the work of God and we are the recipients of His gracious election." (Matthew J. Slick)

In an earlier chapter, we considered the word propitiation (/expiation), and I suggested that it was one of the most confusing aspects that we have dealt with in the book. In this chapter, we turn to what some might justly consider to be the most difficult of the great words of the Christian faith. Certainly, it is a word that I approach, and have always approached, with no little trepidation; only too aware of the difficulties that it raises.

Yet this is not sufficient excuse for avoiding it and, so, we look now at the word 'predestination' – the word that has to do with the Doctrine of Divine Election.

Henry Chadwick points out that "The Jews believed in God's election: God had chosen Israel to be an exclusive society, uncorrupted by heathen influences, yet with the two qualifications that this particularity of providence was not grounded upon any merit in the people chosen but in the sovereign, inscrutable will of God, and that Israel was called to exercise a priestly function in relation to mankind as a whole." (The Early Church; Penguin; 1993; p.9).

So we see the call of Abram; the choice of Isaac over Ishmael; the choice of Jacob over Esau; etc., etc. All through the Tanakh (the Old Testament))we can find clear evidence of this elective process on the part of Almighty God.

In the Old Testament, God the Creator is presented as "... personal, powerful, and purposeful." and we are assured that "... as His power is unlimited, so His purposes are certain of fulfilment." "He is Lord of every situation; ordering and directing everything towards the end for which He made it; and determining every event, great or small, from the thoughts of kings, and the premeditated words and deeds of all men, to the seemingly random fall of a lot."

"The New Testament writers take for granted the Old Testament faith that God is the Sovereign Lord of events, and rules history for the fulfilling of His purposes. Their uniform insistence that Christ's ministry and the Christian dispensation represented the fulfilment of Biblical prophecies, given centuries before, and that God's ultimate aim in inspiring the Hebrew Scriptures was for the instruction of Christian believers, all point to this fact. A new development, however, is that the idea of election now applied, not to national Israel, but to Christian believers as individuals." (see New Bible Dictionary, *in loc*).

As we think together at this whole concept, I want to guide our thoughts, first of all, to the plan of election which we find in, among other passages, Rom.8:29-30. There, Paul is speaking of those whom God has

"*... called according to His purpose for them*" (v.28).

And he writes:

> "*For God knew His people in advance, and He chose them to become like His Son, so that His Son would be the firstborn among many brothers and sisters. And having chosen them, He called them to come to Him. And having called them, He gave them right standing with Himself. And having given them right standing, He gave them His glory.*" (vvs. 29-30).

So we discover that election, predestination, is of God – an expression of His sovereign will; His divine good pleasure. It is a plan, conceived by God from before the foundation of the world that ensures that there would be a positive response, on the part of some, to the saving work of Jesus, the Christ, on the Cross. There are no conditions to be met – all is of God's grace. He it is Who calls, freely and undeservedly, and Who then treats me, just as if I'd never sinned; that I might, one day, be brought to glory; conformed, at last, to the perfect image of the Son.

And, even as we look at the plan of election, we begin to see something of the purpose of election.

The immediate purpose is, as we have just said in different words the salvation of those chosen by God. But this is not all. Listen to Peter:

> "*Peter, an apostle of Jesus Christ, to the exiles of the Dispersion in Pontus, Galatia, Cappadocia, Asia, and Bithynia, chosen and destined by God the Father and sanctified by the Spirit for obedience to Jesus Christ, ...*" (I Peter 1:1-2).

That is to say that the purpose of election is also that there be those who are obedient to Jesus; whose wills submit to His.

And Paul, writing to the disciples of Jesus in Ephesus, has this to say:

> "*All praise to God, the Father of our Lord Jesus Christ, who has blessed us with every spiritual blessing in the heavenly realms because we are united with Christ. Even before He made the world, God loved us and chose us in Christ to be holy and without fault in His eyes. God decided in advance to adopt us into His own family by bringing us to Himself through Jesus Christ. This is what He wanted to do, and it gave Him great pleasure. So we praise God for the glorious grace He has poured out on us who belong to His dear Son.*" (Eph.1:3-7; NLT).

This is the highest purpose of electing grace – the pleasure, the glory, of God; and all else is subservient to it.

Those who are

> "*... in Christ have been destined and appointed to live for the praise of his glory.*" (Eph.1:12-13)

writes Paul, later in the same letter – and all service or good works must always be secondary to this high and lofty purpose.

The plan of election; the purpose of election; and the problems of election. Because, of course, there are problems! You see, if there is election, then it follows – at least to human logic – that there must be rejection! If two people apply to me for a job, and I can only elect, or accept, one of them, then I must necessarily reject the other. Now, if God elects some to salvation is He not, therefore electing the rest to damnation? This was certainly the view of John Calvin who says, in his "Institutes of the Christian Religion" that "All are not created on equal terms, but some are preordained to eternal life, others to eternal damnation; and, accordingly, as each has been created for one or other of these ends, we say that he has been predestinated to life, or death." (Vol.II, p.206). That Calvin was deeply conscious of the seriousness of this doctrine is perfectly evident from the fact that he speaks of it as a "dreadful decree". Nevertheless, as a more modern theologian points out, "... he did not feel free to deny what he regarded as an important Scriptural truth."

The problem is there; the difficulty is real; and what may be said in order to vindicate the God Who is Love (I Jn.4) in this instance? Well, of course, it is highly presumptuous for any mortal being to seek to vindicate the Almighty – rather like seeking to defend a raging lion, as Spurgeon is reported to have said in a different context! But it may help our own understanding of the matter if we remember a number of things. First of all, we remember that

> "... *since all have sinned and fall short of the glory of God, ...*" (Rom.3:23),

then all deserve eternal death and damnation! We recall the parable of Jesus recorded in Matt. 20, about the landowner who hired men early in the morning to work in his vineyard and who, at later times in the day, hired others also. Then, at the end of the day, he paid exactly the same wage to those who had worked only an hour, as had been agreed with, and was paid to, those who had worked all day. The latter, not unnaturally, grumbled.

> "'*Those people worked only one hour,*' *they said,* '*and yet you've paid them just as much as you paid us who worked all day in the scorching heat.*' *He answered one of them,* '*Friend, I haven't been unfair! Didn't you agree to work all day for the usual wage? Take your money and go. I wanted to pay this last worker the same as you. Is it against the law for me to do what I want with my money? Should you be*

jealous because I am kind to others?'" (Matt.20:12-15; NLT).

Now, the parable wasn't told in order to teach any lesson about predestination, and so it isn't a full analogy. But one major point is relevant – none of us receives any less than we deserve, and if Almighty God, in His generosity and grace, wishes to give something more to those whom He chooses, does He not have the right to do so?!

But it is a problem. And it raises other problems. The problem of the necessity of mission. If some are elected, and bound to be saved, why bother with mission? Why not just leave it all to God? The answer, of course, is that it is at the Lord's own command that we seek to share the Gospel message with others.

And there is the problem of human responsibility. If I am not one of the elect, how can I be held responsible for not having accepted Jesus Christ as my personal Saviour and Lord? Paul anticipates that one in his letter to the church in Rome!

> *"Who are you, a mere human being, to argue with God? Should the thing that was created say to the one who created it, "Why have you made me like this?" When a potter makes jars out of clay, doesn't he have a right to use the same lump of clay to make one jar for decoration and another to throw garbage into?"* (9:20-21).

Unfortunately, there is no trite and easy answer to such questions. But there is, I believe, **an** answer. It's an answer that has to do with the whole concept of time and eternity (see Chap.25) – which is why it isn't easy, and certainly isn't trite!

Our human minds tend to think of time in a purely linear fashion. That is to say, we think of time as a straight line with the past at one end; the future at the other; and us, at a point on the line which we refer to as the present. In that picture, Father God is seen as being at the beginning of time, arbitrarily choosing some to salvation, and the rest to damnation, in the classic interpretation of predestination.

However, what we often forget is that time, itself, is a created entity – created by God. It has a definite beginning, and a definite end – ask any reputable scientist since the time of Einstein! Now, it follows that God is, in fact, outwith time! He is the one Who sees all of time – simultaneously! For Him, there is no past, present, and future. All is 'Now'! This is why He told Moses that His Name is "*I AM Who I AM*" (Ex.3:14). That's why the Son could say

"*Before Abraham was even born – I AM*"! (Jn.8:58).

Not "I was" – a statement that would have only have indicated an amazingly long human life, but "I AM"!

Imagine, if you will, a long procession – perhaps the annual London Lord Mayor's Parade. I am standing at the roadside watching the whole spectacle. I see the first band march by. I watch as the first floats are driven past. I clap as the majorettes step high with batons twirling. I look to my left – that first band has long disappeared. I look to my right, and can anticipate some of the spectacle that is yet to pass me – but I don't know exactly what will be coming.

That is an illustration of time. I am at my position in the present. The part of the parade that has passed me is the past. That which has still to arrive is the future. I know what has happened – but it's gone; I know what is happening – it's in front of me; I can only speculate as to what will happen – and I may get it completely wrong.

Now, imagine that you are a reporter for one of the local radio stations. You are reporting on the parade; you're telling your listeners what is happening. The station has chartered a helicopter to fly you 1,000 feet above the parade. From your particular vantage point, you can not only see the bit of the parade that I am able to see at ground level; you are able to see the whole parade. Simultaneously, you are able to see the first marching band, the final float, and everything in between.

Almighty God, from His vantage point of eternity, sees all of time simultaneously. It's not that He is somewhere in the past making choices. It's more that He sees every choice that we make, and sees all of those choices at the same "time"! He knows, in eternity, before I am even born, everything that I will do – every word I will speak; every action I will take; every choice I will make; every thought I will think – in the time-space continuum in which I live out my earthly life.

Now, that may merely have left you more confused than ever! In that case, I would suggest that we must fall back on the realisation that there are certain things that are, quite simply, beyond our comprehension; and trust that an all-wise and all-loving God will not do anything that is unjust, but that His ways are righteous – and will, ultimately, be seen and acknowledged by all, so to be. As Abraham pointed out, so long ago,

> "*Shall not the Judge of all the earth do right?*" (Gen.18:25).

However, there is one final point. We have considered the plan of election, and the purpose of election; and we have looked at some of the problems of election. But we must never forget the privilege of election. That's really what the rest of that 8th chapter of Romans is all about.

> *"So now there is no condemnation for those who belong to Christ Jesus."* (v.1).
>
> *"And we know that God causes everything to work together for the good of those who love God and are called according to his purpose for them."* (v.28).
>
> *"If God is for us, who can ever be against us?"* (v.31).

You see, the elect receive

> *"... the spirit of sonship"* (v.15).

They become

> *"... children of God, and if children, then heirs, heirs of God and fellow heirs with Christ, provided we suffer with Him in order that we may also be glorified with Him."* (vs.16-17).

What a wonderful privilege this is! That by the free and gracious act of God, we might know the riches of His grace!

"Behold, the amazing gift of love the Father hath bestowed on us, the sinful sons of men – to call us sons of God!" (Isaac Watts).

The plan of election – God's plan, whereby He brings some to a full knowledge of salvation;

The purpose of election – that Jesus might be

> *"the firstborn* (pre-eminent) *among many brothers and sisters"* (Rom.8:29; NLT);

that the elect might be obedient to Him; that God might be glorified;

The problems of election – real problems to which there are no nice easy answers; problems of election to damnation, of the need for evangelism, of human responsibility, of understanding the relationship between time and eternity;

The privilege of election – being a true child of God, and joint-heir with Jesus Christ; knowing that, in all things, He is working out that which is best for His people.

So, who are the elect? Well, this is the real paradox. Because the only way in which I can be sure that I am one of the elect is by accepting, in penitence and faith, the Lord Jesus Christ as my Saviour and Lord. In other words, I am assured that I am one of the elect – by becoming one!

This is, indeed, a great mystery. Suffice it to say that God the Holy Spirit only works in the elect; and that if He is prompting you right now, then it is in order that you might claim your inheritance. And if He is speaking to your heart, don't try to chase Him away! Yield your all, and be filled with that wonderful assurance that

> *"You have not chosen Me, but I have chosen you"* (John 15:16).

Predestination: one of the most difficult of the great words of the Christian faith. But for those who have placed their trust in Christ one of the most comforting as they realise that they have been chosen from before the foundation of the world. May each one of us have that full assurance, to the eternal praise of God's glory.

Chapter 16

HOPE

"God is the only One Who can make the valley of trouble, a door of hope" (Catherine Marshall)

As I was working on this chapter, one of the major news items was of thirty-three Chilean miners who had been trapped in a mine, some 2,300 feet below the surface of the ground. After a cave-in at about 1,100 feet, they had already been trapped for about seventeen days before it was discovered that they were alive. The news, then, was that it could take up to four months to rescue them. Relatives had soon gathered in the area around the minehead, in a makeshift camp that they named "Camp Hope". I was reminded of missionary friends who, in 2005, spent six weeks in Pakistan where they were involved in the post-earthquake relief programme – one in organising building of semi-permanent shelters, other as nurse. One of items that they brought back was a book that had been published shortly after the earthquake struck. It was entitled "Paradise Lost" – nothing to do with the well-known work by Milton, but a reference to the fact that, due to its great natural beauty, part of the earthquake zone was known as "Paradise". The book was mostly pictures, but one of the comments was that "A ray of hope can brighten the darkest of hours".

My friends also showed us some of their own photographs of some of the local people whom they met on their arrival – people who were downcast, dejected, filled with despair. Then, even as they were just being questioned in order to properly assess the situation, a change in attitude could be seen. Now, after some seven weeks, someone was showing an interest; someone was actually helping. And this new situation gave new hope. "A ray of hope can brighten the darkest of hours."

My mind also went back to the first time that I preached on this subject. We had experienced a very severe winter, and the north of Scotland was particularly badly affected by heavy snowfalls and severe drifting. One of the main roads was blanketed so quickly that a number of cars were totally engulfed and, when rescuers eventually reached them, the occupants of most of them were dead. However, one gentleman had survived. He had had the good sense, if my memory serves me well, to open a window and push something up through the snow in order to ensure a supply of air. He was a commercial traveller, and was carrying a considerable amount of the items he was promoting. Fortunately for him this was ladies clothing, and he had wrapped himself in nylon garments to keep himself warm. However, when he was finally rescued, he put his survival down to one important factor. He said, "I never lost hope!"

One writer has pointed out, "People view hope very differently. For Henry Miller it was 'a bad thing'. Emil Brunner on the other hand could write: 'What oxygen is to the lungs, such is hope to the meaning of life.' Miller seems to have been criticising the type of hope that refuses to face up to reality, allowing us to live in some kind of dream world. Brunner was identifying the kind of hope that gives meaning and purpose to life, even in the midst of difficulty and disappointment." (Rob James, *Inspire* magazine, April, 2011).

Most folk are familiar with the old saying, "Where there's life there's hope". I would suggest that the experience of my friends, and of the people they went to Pakistan to help; the experience of the Chilean miners; the experience of that commercial traveller; and the experience of many others; suggests that there is another side to that old adage – that it is also true to say that "Where there's hope, there's life"?

A sick person; a hard-pressed man; a nation with its back to the wall; can all continue to fight while hope remains. But if hope is abandoned, any cause is lost. To face each day without hope is, I would suggest, to have lost the battle before it begins.

Of course, to some folk, hope is something with no more to it than the unfounded assertion of Charles Dickens' Mr Micawber that "something will turn up" – what Rob James was suggesting was Henry Miller's type of hope that refuses to face up to reality; allowing us, rather, to live in some kind of dream world. But God's Word provides deeper meaning of word. Leon Morris writes: "... the Scriptural view of hope is of something which is a certainty because it is always grounded in the divine nature and the divine promises." (I & II Thessalonians, Tyndale Press, 1966, p.139). The assertion of Dean Inge, an author less well-known than either Dickens, Milton, Miller, Morris, or Brunner, that "Hope, as a moral quality, is a Christian invention", may not be totally accurate, but it is certainly a Biblical concept. It was from Judaism and the Old Testament. that Christianity inherited this good hope; this God-based, expectant outlook on future time.

Hope was the very life of Israel. Jeremiah speaks of YHWH as being

> "*the* **Hope** *of Israel*" (17:13);

and Joel says that YHWH is

> "*a **Hope** (refuge) to His people*" (3:16).

The Psalms, too, are full of such references.

> "*And now, Lord, for what do I wait?*"

cries David,

> "*My **hope** is in Thee!*" (39:7).

And, towards end of Psalter, another of psalmists declares

> "*Happy is he whose help is the God of Jacob; whose **hope** is in YHWH, his God.*" (146:5).

Even in that most mournful of books, the Lamentations of Jeremiah, the prophet is able to burst out

> "*YHWH is my portion, says my soul, therefore I will **hope** in Him*". (3:24).

Then, when we move into the New Testament, we find belief that the prophecies have been fulfilled; the promised kingdom is at hand; the promised Messiah has come in the Person of Jesus of Nazareth.

The world into which Jesus was born was, in many ways, a world not unlike our own – an age in which, for many, hopes had fallen, faith had been lost. But the New Testament writers show that, in Jesus, hope has been renewed and restored. So, the whole of the Bible speaks of this "divine hope", and we're going to look at just three of the pictures of hope that may be found within its pages.

We begin by noting that hope liberates – it is a door. Through the mouth of His prophet, Hosea, the Lord said to His people,

> "*I will ... make the Valley of Achor a door of **hope**.*" (2:15).

The Valley of Achor was the place at which Achan and his family and flocks were put to death after Achan had stolen, from Jericho, some of the items which had been devoted to YHWH (Josh. 6 & 7). Yet this place, that spoke of Achan's sin and shame, and of the resulting defeat of the Israelites at Ai, was the very place which the Lord gave to His people as a door of hope.

How often God points us back to our Valley of Achor; to the place where we have already failed and fallen. And He says, "There's your door of hope. Go back, and try again." And those who go back, in His strength, are enabled to write a new memory upon the old shame. As has often been said, "Our God is the God of the second chance".

The word *Achor* means *trouble*, and this can us point to a second lesson here. For it's a great thing for us when we have learned that, even in what we experience as trouble, the Lord can be providing, for His children, a door of hope.

"*All things work together for good,*"

wrote Paul,

"*to those who love God.*" (Rom.8:28).

And how many a devout servant of the Lord Jesus owes the beginning of a new and deeper allegiance to the Lord to a serious illness; to some crippling disappointment; to an overwhelming sorrow?! Many have been able to say, again with the Psalmist, that

"*It is good for me that I was afflicted.*" (119:71).

There is a door of hope, even in the valley of trouble, and those who tread it in company with the Lord, will not fail to find it.

And even at the end.

> *"Even 'though I walk through the valley of the shadow of death* (the valley of deep darkness; the valley of trouble), *I fear no evil;"* Why? *"...for Thou art with me; Thy rod* (discipline) *and Thy staff* (protection) *they comfort me.* (they are the source of my strength.)" (Ps.23:4).

With God beside us, there is always this wonderful hope. So Paul could write to the believers in Thessalonica who were concerned about the fate of those of their number who had died, that the survivors should

> *"not grieve, as others do, who have no **hope**."* (1 Thess.4:13).

The hymn-writer proclaims: "All my hope on God is founded" And the more modern song affirms that "My hope is in You, Lord." And it is His love and mercy and faithfulness that **provide** the foundation of our hope. When hope is present, He is not far off. When hope is absent, then He is unrecognised – and we are not only without hope, but without God. It was over the entrance to that godless Inferno of which he wrote, that Dante saw painted the words "All hope abandon, ye who enter here." (The Divine Comedy: *Inferno*; Canto III). Of course, there is another side to this particular coin, that may be seen in the words of a nurse in the A & E Department of a General Hospital who, as she surveyed the physical wreckage resulting from a major road accident, asked "How could I serve in a place like this if the great Hope of the world were a lie?"

Hope is a liberating door, freeing us from defeat and despair. And those who claim to have placed their trust in, and to have surrendered and committed our lives to, Jesus the Christ should through His ultimate victory, be able to hope even when others have **lost** hope.

Hope liberates – it is a door; and hope protects – it is a helmet.

Hope is part of the armour of the Christian, protecting him from danger. Paul, writing again to the Thessalonian believers, says

"...*let us be sober, and put on the breastplate of faith and love and, for a helmet, the hope of salvation.*" (I Thess.5:8).

If we have, and keep, faith in Jesus; if our hearts are set with confidence on that consummation of salvation that He will bring to His own at His return; if we can cry out with the ringing tones of absolute certainty:

"*I know Whom I have believed, and am totally convinced that He is able...*"; (II Tim.1:12)

then we need fear no evil. No foe can touch us –

"*If God be for us, who can be against us?*" (Rom.8:31).

The forces of evil are mighty, but the Lord is on the side of His people.

"*He Who is in you,*"

wrote the aged apostle John to his children in Christ,

"*is greater than he who is in the world.*" (I John 4[4]).

Our spirits may be distressed when we see the apparent power, and the arrogance, of the world but, echoing down the ages, comes the clarion call of the righteous:

"*Hope in God.*" (Ps.42:5,11).

One of the social reformers of an earlier age, John Howard, said, "There is a hope set before me. In the Lord Jesus Christ I put my trust. In many instances God has disappointed my fears and exceeded my hopes." And Edward Mote expresses the same truth in the words of the hymn: "My hope is built on nothing less than Jesus' blood and righteousness."

The man who has lost hope, has tried to build on something else. He must learn to say: "On Christ, the solid Rock, I stand; all other ground is sinking sand." Because the man who can say that; the man – or woman – whose trust is in Christ, and in Him alone; is wearing a tried and trusty helmet which, like the whole armour of God, will enable the wearer

> "*to withstand in the evil day and, having done all, to stand.*" (Eph.6:13).

As the old chorus reminds us: "God is still on the throne, and He will remember His own." In spite of the attempts of governments, dictators, employers, or whoever, righteousness and justice shall not vanish. The Lord will never leave nor forsake His people. And the pledge of that is on a hill outside a city wall where, in the Persona of the Son, Almighty God died the death that man deserved – and deserves! But death could not hold Him. And so He rose, victorious, triumphant, the Conqueror, the One Who alone can give us this blessed hope. When the shallow hopes of the world are all dead, we can hope on in God. And such hope is a bulwark against the wiles of the devil; such hope is a helmet, guarding and protecting the wearer.

Hope liberates – it is a door; hope protects – it is a helmet; and hope holds – it is an anchor.

Listen to the writer of the Letter to the Hebrew believers:

> "*...when God desired to show more convincingly to the heirs of the promise the unchangeable character of His purpose, He interposed with an oath, so that through two unchangeable things, in which it is impossible that God should prove false, we who have fled for refuge might have strong encouragement to seize the hope set before us. We*

have this as a sure and steadfast anchor of the soul, a hope that enters into the inner shrine behind the curtain, where Jesus has gone as a forerunner on our behalf, ..." (Heb.6:17-20).

What is that anchor? What is that hope? The unchangeable character of God. And as long as a man has that hope in his heart, life cannot destroy him. It may hurt him, but it won't be able to break him. As long as that hope holds out, he will weather the roughest storm. That hope is an anchor, sure and steadfast and immoveable; it is the attitude of the one who has gazed upon the face of God the Father, as He has revealed Himself in Jesus –

"...*the same yesterday, today, and forever.*" (Heb.13:8).

In days of brightness, hope can be the sail that the spirit spreads to catch the favouring breeze; a sail that carries the ship over a sunlit sea towards a sure haven. But in the dark night of the storm, hope is an anchor that plunges down through the heaving waters and holds, so firmly, to the Rock beneath – the Rock that is Christ Himself – that not all the fury of the wildest storm that may affect the human life, can drive the vessel from its place of safety.

It's so easy to sing, with great gusto, that:

"We have an anchor that keeps the soul
steadfast and sure while the billows roll.
Fastened to the Rock that cannot move;
grounded, firm and deep, in the Saviour's love." (Priscilla Owens).

But do we really have it? Do you?! Such is the hope that comes with believing faith in the Lord, Jesus Christ: hope that is anchor of the soul fixed, not on any earthly gods, or position, or power, but on the eternal truths, within the veil, behind the embroidered curtain that is spread between mortality and reality, the curtain that has, indeed, been replaced by Jesus,

"...*the new and living way*". (Heb.10:20).

Max Lucado writes: "Hope is not what you expect; it is what you would never dream. It is a wild, improbable tale with a pinch-me-I'm-dreaming ending. ... It's Moses standing in the promised land not with Aaron or Miriam at his side, but with Elijah and the transfigured Christ. It's Zechariah left speechless at the sight of his wife Elizabeth, gray-headed and pregnant. And it is the two Emmaus-bound pilgrims reaching out to take a piece of bread only to see that the hands from which it is offered are pierced.

"Hope is not a granted wish or a favour performed; no, it is far greater than that. It is a zany, unpredictable dependence on a God Who loves to surprise us out of our socks and be there in the flesh to see our reaction." (*God Came Near: Chronicles of the Christ*).

Hope. A concept with which each one of us is familiar; something that we dare not lose. But what sort of hope do you have? The worldly sort: uncertain; vague; sometimes desperate, even despairing; desire with only a faint possibility of fulfilment? Or do you have a God-given hope – inspired by the Father; founded on the Son; sustained by the indwelling power of Holy Spirit – that hope that is complete assurance?

That hope is yours, just for the asking. And you may have it today, simply by letting God into the driving-seat; by giving Him complete control. Then you will know that liberation, that protection, that firm grip. Then you'll stop merely existing, and start real living. For, you see, it's only where there's Christian hope that there's real life at all!

Chapter 17

COVENANT

"... I will remember the covenant I made with you when you were young, and I will establish an everlasting covenant with you."
(Ezek 16:60-61; NLT)

A promise", my late mother would have insisted, "should never be broken!" And I imagine that the vast majority of people would agree with her. Having said that, most people would also accept that, in certain circumstances, a promise may actually **have** to be broken.

For example, I may have promised to meet with someone, perhaps to have a lovely meal at my expense. We arrange that we will meet outside the particular restaurant that I have selected, at 7.00 p.m. on the chosen date. My friend, who has never eaten in such an up-market establishment before, is there at 6.30 p.m. I am not – but that is not a problem. The arrangement is for 7.00 p.m. At 6.45 p.m., I still haven't arrived; nor at 6.55 p.m. The appointed hour strikes – but there is still no sign of me! Perhaps the traffic was particularly heavy on my way to our meeting! Perhaps I have had difficulty in finding a parking place! Perhaps I'll appear around the corner even while these thoughts are racing through my friend's head! Perhaps ... ... !!! By 7.30 p.m., my friend has given up, and returned home – disappointed; perhaps disillusioned; possibly disgusted that I should have broken my promise. It may even be that my friend will never trust me again, but that's as far as it can go. Breaking a promise is not (yet!) considered to be a crime; I won't have the local constabulary at my door with an arrest warrant! Of course, it may well be that there was, indeed, a perfectly valid reason for my not appearing at the rendezvous. My friend may later discover that my car was involved in a serious road traffic incident, and that I am lying in the local hospital with life-threatening injuries! But, regardless of the circumstances, a promise may be broken with, in legal terms, total impunity.

However, let's take a different scenario. Some years ago, my wife and I decided to have a false ceiling installed in our bedroom (it was an old house with very high ceilings!). We arranged for a number of tradesmen to provide quotations for the work, and we made our choice. We entered into a contract by which the tradesman we had chosen agreed to attend to the work, to my specifications; and I agreed to pay to him the sum of money on which we had settled.

The gentleman, and his helper, arrived on the appointed day and within a few hours, the job was completed. Now, imagine that I then had said to him that I didn't have the money to pay him! Does anyone honestly think that he would have told me not to worry; that he had had nothing else to do that day, and the materials were all lying in his workshop just waiting to be used? Of course not. I had not merely made a promise. I had, in Scottish law, entered into a contract – even 'though no formal written agreement had been signed. And so, that gentleman would have had every right to take me to court in order to obtain that which was rightfully his! A contract is a much more serious affair than a promise.

Just over forty years ago (at the time of writing), I stood, rather nervously, in front of the Rev George B. Duncan, at the front of the church building of St.George's-Tron Parish Church, in the lovely city of Glasgow. Adam Hair, the organist, started to play the beautiful *Largo* from George Frideric Handel's cantata, *Xerxes* and, as I looked around, an absolute vision in white came walking up the aisle on the arm of her father. On that day, my fiancée and I took the final step of commitment as Mr Duncan married us to one another "in the sight of God, and before these witnesses."

Now, if we had been married in the local Registry Office, the legality of our union would have been no less. But all that we would have done would have been to enter into a contract, with the implicit understanding that either of us could break it. However, what we actually did was to enter into a covenant relationship, that may be defined as **a special, and solemn, agreement between two people, in which God is involved, and which only God may break**!

The Bible contains a number of covenants. The Old and New Testaments are two covenants. In the Old Testament the Hebrew word *berith* is always translated as 'covenant'. It is often used with the verb *karath*, which means 'to cut'. So, one 'cuts a covenant' rather than 'makes a covenant'. This, in turn, refers to the cutting or dividing of animals into two parts, and the contracting parties passing between them, in entering into a covenant (cf. Gen 15; Jer 34:18,19).

The corresponding word in the New Testament Greek is *diatheke*. In the Authorized Version, the quatro-centenary of which is being celebrated as I draw near to the completion of this little volume, it is generally rendered "testament". However, it ought to be rendered – as it is in some later translations – as "covenant", just as the word *berith* of the Old Testament.

Within the pages of the Old Testament, we may find God's covenant with Adam; with Noah; with Abraham; with Moses, and the Children of Israel; and with David – to name the more significant ones. In these covenants, it is God Who determines the terms – the other party/parties may only accept, or reject, them. In other words, they were akin to Hittite suzerainty treaties, in which there was a senior and a junior party; not parity treaties which were formed between equals.

This is exactly the same in the New Covenant (*he kaine diatheke*). Leon Morris writes, "The underlying Hebrew gives us the meaning of *diatheke*. It indicates that the word signified a transaction between two parties in which one party held the decisive position, laid down the conditions of the agreement and, in general, imposed his will; the sole function of the other party being to accept, or reject, what was determined by the dominant partner." (*The Apostolic Preaching of the Cross*; p.87).

The Old Covenants were all covenants of law. The New Covenant is a covenant of grace. The covenants demonstrate the relationship that Almighty God is prepared; willing; eager to have with each one of us. And, in a Christian context, the New Covenant is nowhere expressed more clearly, simply, and succinctly than in the Covenant meal. This is the time when disciples of Jesus, in obedience to His own command, remember His sacrificial death. (see I Cor.11:24, 25).

The meal in which Jesus and His inner band of disciples partook on that evening before His crucifixion was, of course, a Passover meal. It was a reminder of the covenant-keeping character of YHWH. It was celebrated by divine command, and commemorated the miraculous deliverance of the Children of Israel from Egypt, under the leadership of Moses. That was a deliverance from human, physical, slavery. The deliverance under the New Covenant, celebrated in The Lord's Supper/Communion/the Eucharist, was to be from the very power, penalty and, ultimately, presence of sin itself.

That simple meal is, of course, an enacted sermon. It is a message that explains in the simplest, yet most profound, terms that covenant relationship that Father God desires to have with His adopted children.

When we gather around that Table, we find certain specific things displayed there. We find simplicity. Two simple elements are set before us – bread and wine (frequently today, in my experience, non-alcoholic). The bread is to be broken; the wine is to be poured out.

That the 'breaking' of the bread and the 'pouring out' of the wine are of, at least, equal importance to the elements themselves is explained by D.M.Baillie. He reminds us "... of the important fact, often forgotten, that the 'sensible signs' in this sacrament consist not only of the elements, the bread and the wine, but also of the actions, including the words spoken; but neither the words nor the elements as apart from the actions." (*The Theology of the Sacraments*, p.94). Dr Baillie then goes on to cite P.T. Forsyth from his book *The Church and the Sacraments*, as maintaining "... that in the original Last Supper it was not so much the bread as the breaking; not so much the elements as the actions; that were symbolic."

Simplicity is displayed at the Covenant Table – simple elements, and simple actions; bread broken, wine poured out. Any additions to the Lord's Table are ours. It is, of course, right and fitting that we should give the very best that we have in the service and worship of Almighty God; yet all of the traditional furnishings – silver, or carved wood, trays – are somehow out of place when viewed in the setting of the Upper Room. When we get right down to the basic teaching of the Scriptures, there is a simplicity that is found in what is displayed at the Lord's Covenant Table.

However, we must not forget the significance of what is found displayed there. The bread – to be broken; the wine – to be poured out; are together designed to recall to us the Person, and the Passion, of the Lord Jesus. The person who is leading in the act of Communion may speak and, under God, those words may help those who are listening. But in the actual celebration there is no preacher save the elements, and the actions, and the words of the sacrament – and these alone are sufficient to focus our thoughts on the Christ, and on His death.

So, when we gather around the Table of the New Covenant, we find that it is the Christ Who is displayed there – in His simplicity, and His sufficiency; ready to meet all of our needs.

But if that is what – or, more accurately, Who – is displayed at the Table, we must also ask what it is that is desired there? After all, when we come to a spread table, we obviously want something. And it is equally obvious that the one who has spread that table wants to give us something. A meal is not prepared just for the fun of it (and I speak as one whose early working life was as a professional chef!), but for people; for guests, for customers, even for oneself. As we think of what is desired when we come to the Covenant Table, we must surely consider the guests – guests with hands that are willing to receive. The elements (the bread and the wine) are there to be given – and received! And as those elements are received, physically, so the Christ is received spiritually. The two actions go hand-in-hand, and should never be separated. This is all symbolic of the covenant relationship between the Saviour and His disciples. And this means that there must be, not only hands that are willing to receive, but also hearts that are willing to respond. This is what Father God wants – grateful hearts.

"Rend your hearts, and not your garments",

He had said to His people of old, through the prophet Joel (2:13); while in John's first letter to the early church, we find that wonderful statement that

"*we love Him – because He first loved us.*" (4:19).

Our love is a response to that which He has already shown to us.

But does John's writing of those words in the first century mean that God's command through the prophets is being displayed in the twenty-first? Sadly, it must be said that in many congregations and fellowships in the "West", this is not necessarily the case. Indeed, just as the complaint of the prophets was that Israel had become so familiar with the rituals of her religion that worship had no more than a superficial meaning; so, I fear, many who claim to be disciples of Jesus have become so familiar with the Cross that it has lost most – if not all – of its wonder! Thus, while we receive all that is offered to us, we often come with closed hearts that will not respond.

We come like a child that has been neglected for years and is then brought into the love of a caring family. And when the time comes for that child to celebrate its birthday, it is offered a gift. And it takes the gift. It is willing to receive; but there is no response to the love that the gift symbolises. Of course, we don't even have the excuse of those former years of neglect, for our God has always cared for us. And all that He desires, as those who call themselves by His Name gather around His Table, is guests with hands willing to receive, and hearts willing to respond.

What is displayed at this Covenant Table; what is desired at this Covenant Table; and the third thing to consider involves what is declared at this Covenant Table.

Turning, again, to those familiar words of Paul, we read

"For as often as you eat this bread and drink the cup, you proclaim the Lord's death until He comes." (I Cor.11:26).

And so we find that what is declared here is the action taken by Father God. He has taken the initiative –

"In this is love, not that we loved God, but that He loved us; and sent His Son to pay the penalty for our sins." (I John 4:10).

God has made the first move, and everything has been done for us.

"God shows His love for us in that while we were ye sinners, Christ died for us." (Rom 5:8).

How can fail to love a God like that – a God Who constantly keeps His part of the Covenant into which He has invited us to enter? The hymn-writer was thrilled with this knowledge:

"I've found a Friend; oh, such a Friend!
He loved me – e'er I knew Him."   (James Small).

Prof. John Baillie, somewhere, puts it like this: "It [*the sacrament*] tells, not of something to be accomplished, but of something already accomplished. It is not a programme of moral rearmament it is news about reality. The New Testament does not say, 'Ye shall know the rules, and by them ye shall be bound'; but 'Ye shall know the truth, and the truth shall set you free'. Hence it fundamental proclamation [*or declaration*] is of an action completed; of something that was done, once, and once for all."

The action taken by God. But there is, here, a challenge to you and to me. For that action taken by God demands, from us, an answer - an answer given to God. We come; and we take. But does it stop there? Do we merely keep up a religious habit – and in so doing eat and drink judgement upon ourselves? (see I Cor.11:29). Or do we leave the Table with hearts re-filled with love for our Saviour; eager to go out to renewed service for our Lord; renewed in our commitment to Him, in that Covenant relationship?

Andrew Murray writes: "Let us ask very earnestly whether the lack in our Christian life, and specially in our faith, is not owing to the neglect of the Covenant. We have not worshipped nor trusted the Covenant-keeping God. Our soul has not done what God called us to — "to take hold of His Covenant," " to remember the Covenant"; is it wonder that our faith has failed and come short of the blessing? God could not fulfil His promises in us. If we will begin to examine into the terms of the Covenant, as the title-deeds of our inheritance, and the riches we are to possess even here on earth; if we will think of the certainty of their fulfilment, more sure than the foundations of the everlasting mountains; if we will turn to the God who has engaged to do all for us, who keepeth covenant for ever, our life will become different from what it has been; it can, and will be, all that God would make it." (*The Two Covenants*, PC Study Bible formatted electronic database Copyright © 2003 Biblesoft, Inc. All rights reserved.).

In John Bunyan's great allegorical work, *Pilgrim's Progress*, we read of Christian reaching the Palace Beautiful. There he is welcomed, and given rest and nourishment before being sent on his way to the Celestial city. Each of those who has yielded his/her life to the Lord Jesus; having acknowledged, and confessed, their own sinfulness, and looked to Him alone for their salvation; is travelling to the celestial City – that

> "... *city which has foundations, whose builder and maker is God.*" (Heb 11:10),

prepared for them by Father God (see Heb.11:16). As we come to that Table, renewing and reaffirming our covenant relationship, through Jesus, we also are provided with rest and nourishment before being sent out on the next stage of our personal journeys.

This is all the work of our Covenant-keeping God – Who never lets us down, and Who never lets us go. To Him be all praise, and honour, and glory.

Chapter 18

LOVE

"Three things will last forever—faith, hope, and love—and the greatest of these is love." (I Cor.13:13)

In morally corrupt Corinth, love had become a mixed-up term with little meaning. Today people are still confused about love. Love is the greatest of all human qualities, and it is an attribute – indeed, the very essence – of God Himself. Love involves unselfish service to others; to show it gives evidence that you care. Faith is the foundation and content of God's message; hope is the attitude and focus; love is the action. When faith and hope are in line, you are free to love completely because you understand how God loves.

Love may be considered to be of the utmost importance because it is, first and foremost, the Biblical description of God!

"God is love"

proclaims John in his first pastoral letter (4:8,16). Love, he is saying is the very essence of Almighty God! And the essence of anything is that which makes it what it is. So, in my early days in the catering trade, I knew that if I wanted my custard to have the flavour of vanilla, I had to add some vanilla essence – some of that

173

(the flavour) which made vanilla to be vanilla; that is essential to its being!

It is not to claim too much to say that, without Almighty God, love could not exist! Indeed, we might even say, with all reverence, that without love, God would not exist!

When I was a young student at the Bible Training Institute, in Glasgow, the lecturer in Systematic Theology was Rev John Peck. He used many memorable illustrations as he sought to impart something of his own love for the systematic study of theology to his students. Speaking of love, he would point out that many consider love as a ladder, with God on the top rung – the pinnacle, as it were, of love – and we mere mortals somewhere near the bottom. "This is false." he would say, "God *is* the ladder!"

Many others have written about the four Greek words, each with its own shade of meaning, all of which are translated into the English language by the single word 'love', and I do not intend to repeat such work. Suffice it to say that an understanding of the different words is of great use in clarifying many passages in the New Testament record. One of the most obvious of these is in the 21st chapter of John's account of the Gospel record, and in vs.15-17. This is the passage in which we learn of the threefold question, of the risen Jesus, to Simon Peter. Three times, we read in the English versions, He asked Peter,

"Simon, son of John, do you love me?"

Twice, we read, Peter replied with the words

"Yes, Lord; You know that I love You."

However, when Jesus asked the question a third time, we read that Peter was grieved that he should be asked the question yet again.

Now it may be that you are like I was, and thought that it was merely the repetition of the question that so upset the big fisherman! But that is not the case. The real reason for his displeasure is found in the Greek of the original. On the first two occasions, Jesus asks His question using the word *agapas* – from *agape*, which is the unconditional love that Father God has for you and for me. Yet on each of these occasions, Peter replies using the word *philo* – from *phileo*, which is the word used of a friend for whom one has a deep affection! Then, when Jesus asks the question for the third time, He uses *phileis* – again from *phileo*. And it is this that cuts Peter! It is not the number of times that the question has been asked, but the change in the word. Jesus has asked him if he loves Him, unconditionally. Peter twice replies that he has great affection for the Lord. So, the third time Jesus asks, in effect, "Simon, are you certain that you love me even **that** much?"

Now, to me, one of the wonders of that little incident is that Jesus accepts even Peter's less-than-unconditional love! But we need to understand the different 'levels' of love to fully appreciate that story.

When I was teaching, I sometimes used a particular video-tape with classes. It started off in the studio of Radio 1 with DJ Simon Mayo looking at a number of piles of compact discs. He explained the subject matter of each pile and, when he came to what was, by far, the highest pile, he informed us that the common subject was – love!

Possibly the best-known verse in the whole of the New Testament part of the Bible is the one often referred to as "the Gospel in a nutshell" – John 3:16.

> *"For God so loved the world that He gave His only Son, that whoever believes in Him should not perish but have eternal life."*

The old song tells us that "It's love that makes the world go round" But it speaks only of human love. John 3:16 speaks of love that really does make go, and keep going, the whole of the created universe – even the love of Almighty God.

As we look at John 3:16 we may see, in it, certain characteristics of the love of God. We discover, for instance, that His love is undeserved.

"For God so loved the world ..."

That's a pretty plain statement, that may be understood by anyone But it begs the question – "Why did God love the world?" We might consider the rebelliousness of mankind. At the very beginning, Adam and Eve enjoyed the most intimate presence of Almighty God in the Garden of Eden. But they disobeyed the one restrictive command that had been given to them, by eating of the fruit of the tree of the knowledge of good and evil, and their disobedience allowed sin and death to enter the creation – and cut them off from the near presence of the all-holy One, Who cannot look upon sin.

And then, we read, sin spread until the stage was reached that YHWH

> *"... saw that the wickedness of man was great in the earth and that every imagination of the thoughts of his heart was only evil continually. And YHWH was sorry that He had made man on the earth, and it grieved Him to His heart So YHWH said, "I will blot out man whom I have created from the face of the ground, man and beast and creeping things and birds of the air, for I am sorry that I have made them."* (Gen.6:5-7).

And so God sent a worldwide flood, that destroyed sinful humanity – with the exception of the righteous Noah, who found favour in God's eyes, and also Noah's family.

From Noah, through the patriarchs Abraham, Isaac, and Jacob, were descended the Children of Israel. But, in spite of the wondrous works that YHWH did on their behalf, and the teaching of the prophets whom He sent among them, they were constantly running after "other gods" (Deut.29:26, *inter al*), and rejecting the One true God, the Creator and Sustainer of all that is.

And down to the present time, when that same God – in spite of having revealed Himself supremely in the Persona of the Son (see chap. 22) – is rejected, and neglected by so many, including some of those who appear, on the surface, to be on His side but who offer mere lip-service, one hour per week, at a worship service that has more to do with social respectability and tradition than with a living relationship.

If we were to be treated by others, in the same way that Almighty God is treated by the majority of people in the so-called 'western world', we would feel extremely hard done by! The wonder of the Christian Gospel is that, undeserving as we are, God still loves us.

Paul, in his usual direct way, makes the point to the early Christian believers in the great metropolis of Rome:

> *"While we were still weak, at the right time Christ died for the ungodly. Why, one will hardly die for a righteous man - though perhaps for a good man one will dare even to die. But God shows His love for us in that while we were yet sinners Christ died for us."* (Rom.5:6-8).

Father God didn't even wait until we reached a certain standard before loving us. He loves us in all of our selfishness; our rottenness; our sinfulness. For God's love, and God's salvation, are two different things – although one of the major areas of difficulty in the sharing of the Gospel message in the west today, is the total confusion by so many, of the one with the other!

The wondrous love of God is undeserved. It doesn't depend on any goodness that you or I might have, or on any love that we might manage to show towards Him. Indeed, the apostle points out, so succinctly, that

> "*We love, because He first loved us.*" (I John 4:19).

But not only is the love of God undeserved, it is also unrestrained. You see, it's possible to love in a less than passionate sense. It's possible to practise a form of love that is content to just not harm another; that is 'only' friendship. This is one of the four 'loves' of the Greek language – *phileo*. But God's love is much greater than that. For we read, not only that

> "*God so loved the world ...*",

but also

> "*... that He gave His only-begotten Son ...*"

This tells us something about the cost of God's love; of the length to which He was, and is, willing to go in order to extend that love towards a sinful mankind.

We've already looked at Atonement in chapter 6. But let's take a brief look at some of the reasons given by theologians, through the centuries, as they have endeavoured to explain the death of the Lord Jesus at Calvary.

It was the early Church Father, Origen (c. 185–254) who introduced the theory commonly referred to as the "Ransom to

Satan" theory. Put simply, this suggests that the death of Jesus was a ransom paid to the adversary in order to cancel the just claim that Satan had upon mankind because of Adam's sin. Of course, the difficulty with this theory is that it does, up to a point, put the devil in the driving seat! However, Origen's theory held sway for about a thousand years, until a man named Anselm argued that, since the devil is, himself, an outlaw, he could never have a just claim on humanity. It was, therefore, unnecessary for any ransom to be paid to him.

Anselm (c.1033 – 1109) offered an alternative with his "Satisfaction" theory. He argued that sin consists of a failure to give to God the honour and glory that are His due. This means that mankind has contracted a debt of obligation to the Lord. Because of His holiness, God could not simply 'let us off'; we could not pay the debt ourselves; and so, Anselm proposed, God the Son paid the debt for us. He did this through His perfect obedience – even to the point of dying on the cross. With the debt now satisfied, God the Father was free to show us His mercy; free us from sin; and reconcile us to Himself as we confess our sins, repent, and respond positively to His grace.

Around about the same time as Anselm was putting forward his theory of the atonement, another theologian, and philosopher – Peter Abelard – developed the third major theory that has become known as the "Moral Example" theory. According to Abelard, the life and death of Jesus provide us with a perfect moral example of love, and obedience, and humility – and it is following this example that saves us. However, while this idea may be helpful for practical discipleship (cf. Eph.5:2), it is inadequate for salvation. Indeed, it makes Jesus little more than any person whose life inspires us to live better lives ourselves. But the New Testament makes clear that Jesus, alone, is the basis of our salvation, making Abelard's theory less than satisfactory!

The fourth of the great theories of the atonement is the "Penal Substitutionary" theory, developed by the Reformers, and most clearly taught in the written Word of God. It may be thought of as a modified version of Anselm's Satisfaction theory, with the main difference being that instead of saying that the Lord Jesus paid the debt that we owed, it says that He took the punishment that we deserved. It was in this way that He satisfied the Father's demand for justice, and enabled us to be reconciled fully to Him (cf. II Cor.5:19). This theory also directs our attention "... to that conscious act of man by which he appropriates the righteousness of Christ – the act of faith", while being careful "not to represent faith as the meritorious cause of justification." (Louis Berkhof, *A History of Christian Doctrine*, p.184).

But the basic reason for the atonement is the unrestrained love of God. It was love that took Jesus to the cross – love for you, and love for me. It was love that held Him there, as He suffered, and died, in your place, and mine. The love of God cost Him dearly – but He so loved us, that He gladly paid the price.

Undeserved; unrestrained; and unequalled.

> "*God so loved the world that He gave His only-begotten Son; that whoever believes in Him should not perish, but have eternal life.*"

God's love is unequalled because it, and it alone, offers salvation. But note that well – salvation is offered! It requires a response to God's love – the response of our own love, and obedience, and trust. It is when that response is made that the assurance is given that sin has been forgiven. It is then that the person receives new, spiritual, life – and is filled with a new power for living.

And it must be a personal response! My belief; my trust; are what affect me. The faith of parents, grandparents, spouses, siblings, friends, can never be enough. No individual can appropriate salvation on behalf of another. Here, each of us stands alone. As the title of one of the books on my study shelves reminds us, *God has no grand-children*! Salvation is a personal transaction between each of us, individually, and God.

The love of God – undeserved; unrestrained; unequalled.

> *"God so loved the world that He gave His only-begotten Son; that whoever believes in Him should not perish, but have eternal life."*

Have you believed? Have you responded to His love with the love of your own heart? Have you offered yourself to Him, as a living sacrifice, to be obedient in His service for whatever time you may have on earth?

The story is told of a little girl, playing with her doll while her mum was busy writing a letter. When the mother had finished her task, she turned to her daughter.

"You can come now, Alice. I have done all that I have to do this morning."

The child ran to her mother, exclaiming, "I'm so glad; for I wanted to love you so much."

"But I thought that you were happy with your doll", said the mother.

"Yes, I was," responded the child, "but I soon get tired of loving her, for she can't love me back."

"And is that why you love me?" asked the mother, softly.

"That's one why – but it's not the first and best why." came the answer.

The mother was puzzled! "And what is the first and best why?" she enquired.

The reply was immediate. "Because you loved me when I was too little to love you back."

The mother's eyes, we are told, filled with tears as she remembered, and quietly murmured those words from John's first letter:

> "*We love Him, because He first loved us.*" (4:19).

Take some time to read the well-known passage Isaiah 53:3-6. But whenever it reads 'we', 'our', and 'us', substitute 'I', 'my', and 'me', respectively. And then, just sit quietly and reflect on what you have read!

> "*For God so loved the world that He gave His only Son that whoever believes in Him should not perish but have eternal life.*"

Chapter 19

LOVE (2) – a Case Study

"Christ is the Head of this home;
the unseen Guest at every meal,
the silent Listener to every conversation"

What I want to do, in this chapter, is to take one specific example of love, and use it to flesh out what love is. We find it in a home! But not just any home. This is a home in the village of Bethany, close to the great city of Jerusalem; and it is the home of two sisters and their brother. This is the home of Martha, and Mary, and Lazarus. It was a home in which Jesus found peace and rest amid the turmoil that surrounded Him as He made His way, steadfastly, towards Gethsemane, and Calvary. There, He found love and affection amid the hatred that was being ever more clearly manifest by the Jewish hierarchy. There, He found fidelity and loyalty amid the fickleness and petty arguing of even the inner band of disciples.

It's perhaps worth asking, in a moment of self-examination, how far Jesus would find those qualities in us? If we had lived at that time, would our homes have been places which the Lamb of God would have visited; in which He would have been able to relax, and feel perfectly at home? Are we the sort of people whose company He enjoys today? Prof. Barclay writes, "It is one of the most precious things in the world to have a house and a home into which one can go at any time, and find rest, and understanding, and peace, and love. That was doubly true of Jesus, for He had "nowhere to lay His head" (Lk.9:58). But in the home at Bethany, Jesus did have such a place. There, there were three people who loved Him; and there He could go for rest from the tensions of life." (Daily Study Bible; *in loc*).

As we look at that home, and at the three who lived there, we see that each of them has something to teach us about the love that the Lord Jesus seeks from us. When we look at Martha, who appears to have been the eldest in the family, we see something of the swiftness of love. She was so eager and, surely, to Jesus that would have been so welcome. There was an immediate willingness to be serving and doing – and how that aspect of true love must have attracted Him! Luke records an earlier visit of the Saviour to that home (10:38-42), and tells us of Martha busying herself in the kitchen. Jesus was no sooner over the threshold than she was up – bustling about; serving the Master Whom she loved. The swiftness of love. The great expositor and commentator, Matthew Henry, writes, "Martha's natural temper [temperament/character] was active and busy; she loved to be here, there, and at the end of everything." (Commentary on the Whole Bible; *in loc*).

As Martha responded so swiftly, in love, we may note the demands that she would gladly meet. She was the sort of person who would gladly have accepted – indeed, embraced – the injunction of the Lord as found in Matthew 5:41.

> "... *if anyone forces you to go one mile, go with him two miles.*"

For Martha, to hear was to obey. Anything that Jesus asked her to do would immediately be done – and done, almost to a fault! And Jesus saw, and appreciated, this. Even in that story in Luke 10, the rebuke that He gave was full of gentleness. He repeated her name

"*Martha, Martha*"

or, as we might say, "Dearest Martha". He spoke as One in earnest; One deeply concerned for her welfare. "Dearest Martha! You're getting into a frazzle preparing a five-course dinner for Me, and setting out the best china – when all that I really want is a mug of tea!".

Yet the fact remains that, although on this particular occasion it did not take the most relevant form, Martha's watchword was service – full and willing service. Does the Lord Jesus find that attitude in your life; in mine? Does He turn to us knowing that we won't be content to do the minimum we must, the least with which we can get away; but that we will want to do the maximum we can, the most of which we are capable? Is the response of our love to Him such that His complaint must be that we are doing too much? In the book *Sounds from Heaven* – the story of the revival in the Scottish island of Lewis in 1949-52 – is this profound statement: "Many of us pray just enough to ease the conscience, but not enough to win any decisive victory. We are playing at praying" (p.129). May it be said that too many of us have exactly the same problem with Christian service?!

In Martha's case, there were demands that she would willingly meet, and there was a delight that she would certainly show. We all know folk like that. Their delight in performing a particular task is so obvious – it almost shines from their faces! Martha was of that ilk! She met every demand placed upon her; she delighted to do so; and her enjoyment was patently obvious to all – not least to the Master for Whom she was doing it. And so we read:

"*Now Jesus loved Martha.*"

The swiftness of love – made clear in demands gladly met, and delight clearly shown. Does Jesus get swift, eager, joyous responses from us? This is one of the characteristics that draws and attracts Him. This is why some get bigger, and more responsible, jobs – not from men, but from Father God Himself! He picks those who display a real willingness to serve Him.

But there is a second way in which we can see love being shown in that village home; another aspect of it that Jesus found so attractive. And we may see it as we look at the second member of the family – Mary. What was it that drew the Christ to her?

The name, Mary, is all too common in the pages of the New Testament. But on at least three occasions (Luke 10:39; John 11:2, 32) there is no doubt at all that it is this particular Mary to whom reference is being made. And the striking fact is, that on each of those occasions, Mary is found in the same position –

"... *at His feet.*"

So we may learn that her contribution to the love that Jesus found in that little family had to do with the nearness of love. For, if Martha demonstrated a love that was never idle, then Mary demonstrated a love that was never distant. Just as Martha's desire was to serve, and go on serving; so Mary's desire was to be near – as near as possible; to be

"... *at His feet.*"

How well Mary knew her Master! Her devotion seemed to give her a special insight into His own problems. So, the story is recorded of her anointing him with an expensive perfumed balm, just before His last journey to Jerusalem. (John 1:1-3). And when Judas Iscariot commented on her loving generosity which, he claimed, was a dreadful waste that could have been put to better use, Jesus' own words were, in effect, "Leave her alone! She's the only one who realises what is happening, and is going to happen. This is a situation that is never going to be repeated" (vs.7-8). "The only one who realises"! There was an insight that love would gain in nearness; but there was also a contact that love must make in nearness.

For Mary, it wasn't enough just to know; she had to let Jesus know that she knew – she had to make sure that He knew that she had this special insight.

And this is always true of deep love. I recall, as a child contracting, along with my younger brother, the infectious disease of scarlet fever. In those far-off days, we were placed in an isolation ward in a nearby hospital. Our parents were not allowed to enter the ward, but it was on the ground floor and, the next thing we saw was our mum's face at one of the high windows – standing (we found out, much later) on our dad's shoulders!! She knew that we would be receiving the best care and attention that was available – better than she would have been able to provide for us. But her desire was to be with her children – not for any additional peace of heart that she might have gained, but simply in order that we might know, and be reassured, of her love for us.

The story is told of an Art Gallery, somewhere in The Netherlands. The guide was showing a party of visitors around and they eventually came to a particular representation of the Crucifixion. One of the party complained, rather loudly, that he couldn't see the face of the man on the cross. "Ah, sir," said the guide. "Those who would gaze on His face must first kneel at His feet." We might add that those who would seek to draw near to Him as Mary did; to get to know Him better; must also, like her, spend much time

"at His feet".

The nearness of love. How close, I wonder, are you and I to the mind and heart of the Christ? How much insight marks your service – and mine? And if, in all honesty, we have to admit that we are not particularly close; if we lack genuine insight; may it be that we are simply not spending enough time

"*at His feet*"?

The swiftness of love, shown by Martha. The nearness of love shown by Mary. And then, from the third member of that little household, we find shown what will be, to some, the most encouraging aspect of love. Because, as we look at Lazarus, we see something of the quietness of love.

In John's account of the Gospel record, and in chapters 11 and 12 Lazarus is mentioned frequently. Yet nowhere in those chapters – or, indeed, anywhere else in the pages of God's written Word – is there any record of anything that he said! He was, obviously, like my own late father, a man of very few words.

There are many people like Lazarus in the church today. Men and women to whom the very thought of having to speak in public would be almost enough to bring on a nervous breakdown! Yet although this seems to have been the case with Lazarus, Jesus still loved him – loved him, perhaps, because of his quietness. It is surely not stretching the bounds of imagination too far to think of them, at the end of the day, when the crowds had gone home, just walking through the fields, or sitting outside the house.

It may have been that, for Jesus, there was a silence that He would need. That might be all that He wanted – and Lazarus knew that this was bound to be so at times. Perhaps this was an opportunity for Jesus to speak to someone, outwith the inner circle of disciples without interruption from critics and cynics. Lazarus couldn't say much – but he could listen! And what a help that can be.

Sometimes, when we are deeply involved in the work of the Lord Jesus, things can get a little bit out of perspective. At such times we, too, need someone who will be content just to listen; someone who can view the situation from a slightly different standpoint. I have three particular friends to whom I turn when I have particular decisions to make. They are men whom I trust implicitly; men of maturity, integrity, and spiritual wisdom; men who will listen, and even advise – but never coerce. Now I know, of course, that I can go straight to Jesus. I know that God the Holy Spirit guides and directs. But I'm not always good at recognising His guidance all by myself – and I suspect that I am not alone in that! And so I praise God for providing me with those human friends through whom He so often channels His guidance.

And then, there are the times when we need to be the listener for someone else. Jesus would have found a depth of fellowship with Lazarus that He may not have been able to enjoy with even Peter, and James, and John simply because they were too practically involved in the work with Him.

But would there not also have been a service He would find? Lazarus may have found it difficult to speak to men – but one suspects that he had a lot to say to God. He may not have been a public speaker – but one suspects that he was a man of prayer. And Jesus would have known that. He'd have known that while Lazarus wasn't saying much to Him, he was praying much for Him.

How much each of us owes to those who pray. How much less work would be done in the church, and by the church, if the many faithful men and women of prayer were to desert her. For many, indeed, this is the only real sphere of service that they can find – and it is of prime importance. I've often heard people say that, in a particular situation, "The only thing left to do is to pray". May I suggest that it is the first thing that we should do in any situation, regardless of the circumstances?!

One last point must be made before we leave the subject of love. We have considered the amazing love that God has for each one of us. We have looked at the love that the Lord Jesus should have from us. But, of course, there is a third aspect of love, and that is the love that disciples of Jesus are to display towards one another.

In his first letter to the church at large, the beloved disciple, John, writes:

> "*Beloved, if God so loved us, we also ought to love one another.*" (4:11).

And, a little later on, he writes:

> "*... this commandment we have from Him, that he who loves God should love his brother also.*" (4:21).

To experience the love of God is a gift beyond comparison; to display love for the Lord is a privilege to be grasped; but to love one another is a command to be obeyed!

Of course, it isn't easy to love some people, even within the fellowship of disciples of Jesus. There are those who constantly "rub us up the wrong way". There's a little verse that makes the point quite well:

"To live above with saints we love,
Ah, that is purest glory.
To live below with saints we know,
Well, that's another story!"

That's why we ourselves must remain close to the source of love – the Lord Himself.

Writing his account of the Gospel record, John shares these words of the Lord Jesus:

> "*A new commandment I give to you, that you love one another; even as I have loved you, that you also love one*

another. By this all men will know that you are My disciples, if you have love for one another." (13:34-35).

On my left hand, I wear a wedding ring. It's a gold wedding ring. How may I be assured that it is, indeed, gold and not just some base metal with a golden coating? Because it has a hallmark – and that hallmark is the absolute guarantee that my ring is the genuine article.

Love is the hallmark of the Christian! Love is the assurance that I am His, and that He is mine. It's not my Biblical knowledge; it's not my doctrinal, and theological, orthodoxy; it's not my financial giving. It's my love – for God, and for my brothers and sisters in Christ.

The story is too long to tell in detail, but I recall an occasion on which a preaching invitation had been mixed up, and I discovered that I needed a fresh message in a very short time. I prayed about it, and the Lord kept leading me to I Cor.12-14. The fellowship with which I had been asked to share were not "into" charismatic things, and I tried to find another message – but to no avail. The Lord wouldn't allow me to go anywhere else!

Then I made my (for me!) great discovery! You see, I Cor.12 and 14 have to do with the gifts of God the Holy Spirit. And they are two very important sections of that particular letter. But I Cor.13 is all to do with love! So I realised that (a) love is central; and (b) the gifts are balanced on love. From then on, I looked a little differently at those who claimed to have great gifting. I still do! If you tell me about the great gifts that you exercise, I will look for love. If I am unable to see love – the **fruit** of God the Holy Spirit – I will question the actual source of the **gifts** that you profess!

"If I speak in the tongues of men and of angels, but have not love, I am a noisy gong or a clanging cymbal. And if I

have prophetic powers, and understand all mysteries and all knowledge, and if I have all faith, so as to remove mountains, but have not love, I am nothing. If I give away all I have, and if I deliver my body to be burned, but have not love, I gain nothing." (I Cor 13:1-3).

Love – the very nature of God;

Love – that which the Lord desires to receive from us;

Love – when shown to others, the very hallmark of my Christian life and service.

"Beloved, let us love one another; for love is of God, and he who loves is born of God and knows God." (I John 4:7).

Chapter 20

RAPTURE

"For the Lord Himself will descend from heaven with a cry of command, with the archangel's call, and with the sound of the trumpet of God. And the dead in Christ will rise first; then we who are alive, who are left, shall be caught up together with them in the clouds to meet the Lord in the air; and so we shall always be with the Lord." (I Thess.4:16-17)

The word 'Rapture', like the word 'Trinity' is not to be found anywhere in the pages of the written Word of God. However, again like the Trinity, the concept is clearly shown as an event that will herald the end of time itself. Closely linked to the concept of the Rapture, is that of the Second Coming – also clearly taught in the pages of the New Testament. Part of the difficulty with these two terms – Rapture and Second Coming/Advent – is that there is an understandable confusion as to whether they refer to two separate events, or will take place simultaneously.

My personal position is that they are two separate, and distinct, events; but I would not allow a difference in interpretation on this matter to come between me and a brother/sister in the Lord. Indeed, as I continue to read the Word, and to discuss with others, I find my own position moving in a number of subtle ways!

But if these two events are indeed, different and separate, what are they, and what may we learn about them from the pages of God's written Word?

The Rapture, I believe, is that event that will take place

> "... *in a moment, in the twinkling of an eye, at the last trumpet* [shofar]. *For the trumpet will sound, and the dead will be raised imperishable, and we shall be changed.*" (I Cor.15:52).

It is that event at which

> "... *the Lord Himself will descend from heaven with a cry of command, with the archangel's call, and with the sound of the trumpet* [shofar] *of God. And the dead in Christ will rise first; then we who are alive, who are left,* **shall be caught up together with them in the clouds to meet the Lord in the air;** *and so we shall always be with the Lord.*" (I Thess.4:16-17; *emphasis added*).

The Second Coming/Advent, on the other hand, is when the Lord Jesus will return, with His raptured church, to defeat the antichrist, destroy evil, and establish His millennial Kingdom. Paul refers to this event, also in his First Letter to the church in Thessalonica:

> "*Now may our God and Father Himself, and our Lord Jesus, direct our way to you; and may the Lord make you increase and abound in love to one another and to all men, as we do to you, so that He may establish your hearts unblamable in holiness before our God and Father,* **at the coming of our Lord Jesus with all His saints**." (3:11-13 *emphasis added*).

So, we might say that the basic difference is that, at the Rapture, the Lord meets with His saints in the air, taking them to the marriage supper of the Lamb (Rev.19:9); at the Second Coming – seven years later, from a pre-tribulation perspective – He will return with His saints to the earth, where they will reign with Him through the Millennium.

Those later words of Paul to the Thessalonian believers were in answer to something that was troubling them. They were looking forward to the return of the Lord Jesus, as had been promised (see Acts 1:10-11). But they were concerned about their believing friends who had already experienced physical death. Paul was able to assure them that, at the Rapture that would precede the actual Second Coming, the bodies of those who had died before, and whose spirits had already passed

"through the veil"

(see ch.25), would rise to join with believers who were still physically alive, and that they would all meet with the Lord together –

"in the air"

(the realm in which the satan thinks that he has the power: Eph.2:2).

So, what do Paul's words tell us about the Rapture? He refers, first of all, to the departure we shall make.

> *"... first the Christian dead will rise; then we who are left alive shall join them, caught up in the clouds to meet the Lord in the air."* (I Thess.4:17; NEB).

We will leave this earth, with all of its sin and evil; its pain and heartache; its downright rottenness; its satanic influence on all that is good and true. (cue The Gaither Vocal Band singing *What a Day*!).

We may note the certainty of this departure. In 4:15, Paul says

> "*Here we have a definite message from the Lord*" (Phillips).

No theory; no speculation; no hypothesis that Paul has formed by himself; but a definite "message from the Lord" and, as such, an absolute certainty – something of which we may be completely assured.

Dr Luke records, in Acts 1:11, the words of the angel to the, doubtless mystified, if not terrified, disciples who had just seen their Lord ascend into a cloud:

> "*This Jesus, Who was taken up from you into heaven, will come in the same way as you saw Him go into heaven.*"

So we may be sure that Jesus will return – and Paul provides the assurance that, when He does, His faithful people will depart this earth to be with Him.

Of course, as all of the commentators are quick to point out, Paul did not mean, by the use of "we", that he expected the Rapture to take place within his own mortal lifetime. He says "we" because, at the time of his writing he, Silvanus and Timothy (who were with him – 1:1), and the Thessalonian believers to whom he was writing; all of them were among the believers who were still living on earth. But he immediately modifies his use of the word by, himself, interpreting it to mean "those who are left when the Lord comes" (William Hendriksen; 1&2 Thessalonians; Banner of Truth, London, 1972; *in loc*). Indeed, Hendriksen goes on to suggest that Paul is also making the point, here, that only God knows who will be included in "those"!

Paul knew that there was a strong possibility that the rapture would not take place immediately (see II Thess.2:3). No doubt he hoped that he might live to experience that wonderful event, and he exhorted everyone to conduct themselves in such a way as to always be ready. But he does not set a date, and those who would attempt to do so are either fools who know no better, or among the most arrogant of people. There is only one thing of which we may be certain – and that is that the Rapture will take place.

It will take place with, first of all,

> "*a cry of command*".

What, we must ask, is the command, and to whom is it given? Well, I want to take us back to a home in the village of Bethany – the home of three siblings who were friends of the Lord Jesus: Martha, Mary, and Lazarus. Sadly, Lazarus has died. But Jesus has, at last, arrived. You may read the full story in John 11, but towards the end, we see Jesus, at the tomb from which the stone has been rolled away, and John records:

> "… *He cried with a loud voice, "Laz'arus, come out.*" (v.43).

This was a "*cry of command*" – and if the Lord Jesus had not named Lazarus, then we may wonder how many others would have come out of their tombs!

So, the "*cry of command,*" to which Paul refers, is the command that leads him to write, in the next sentence, that:

> "*the dead in Christ will rise first;*"

It is the command to those who have died "in the Christ" to rise to meet with Him,

"... *in the air* ..."!

It may be given, on this occasion, by an archangel – but the result is still astounding!

A cry of command, and

"... *the sound of the trumpet of God.* ..."

or, I would suggest, more accurately, the sound of the shofar – the ram's horn that was used a long time before metal trumpets had been created. Why a ram's horn? Well it is an instrument that is not made by human hand; it is not a musical instrument on which one may play a melody, but it simply makes a sound; and it was used in Israel on different occasions. For example, when Moses received the Ten Commandments from God on Mount Sinai, the people heard a very loud blast of the shofar. The Children of Israel were commanded to blow the shofar not only on Rosh Hashanah (the Jewish New Year), but also at the beginning of the Jubilee Year. Shofars were also blown by warriors in battle, and by musicians in the Temple.

In the Biblical times of Israel, the shofar was blown for several reasons. Some that are relevant to the Rapture are:

1. To celebrate a simcha (joyous occasion) – for the disciple of Jesus, the Rapture will be a truly joyous occasion;

2. To proclaim liberty to the captives – for the disciple of Jesus, the Rapture will bring about the ultimate freedom from sin;
3. To hail a king at his coronation – for the disciple of Jesus, the rapture will enable us to hail the King of kings as we are unable to do while we inhabit these sinful bodies;
4. To warn of impending judgment – the Rapture will be an unarguable sign that the final judgement is close;
5. To gather troops to battle – there will be a final battle when the Lord Jesus will destroy the forces of evil;

One other thought is given in the Talmud – the set of teachings and commentaries on the Torah (the five books of Moses) that form the basis for Jewish law. It contains the opinions of thousands of Jewish rabbis, from different periods in the history of the Jewish people, after the destruction of the Second Temple in 70 AD. In the Talmud we read: "Rabbi Abbahu said: The Holy One, blessed be He said: Sound before Me a ram's horn so that I will remember on your behalf the binding of Isaac, the son of Abraham, and to account it to you as if you had bound yourselves before me."

In this case, Rabbi Abbahu is claiming that the shofar is an allusion to the ram we read about in the story of the binding of Isaac, which is the Torah reading for Rosh Hashanah. The shofar reminds Jews of the sacrifice Abraham made, and they use it to remind God of that same sacrifice, so that He'll credit their good actions to Jews, today. (Remember, in the end of that story, Abraham sees a ram and sacrifices it instead of Isaac.)

My favourite English-language hymn begins:

"When peace, like a river, attendeth my way.
When sorrows, like sea-billows, roll.
Whatever my lot, Thou hast taught me to say:
"It is well, it is well with my soul."

But the final verse proclaims:

"But Lord, 'tis for Thee, for Thy coming we wait.
The sky, not the grave, is our goal.
Oh trump of the angel, oh voice of the Lord.
Blessed hope, blessed rest for my soul."

Whether we are among those who have died in Christ, or whether we are still inhabiting these mortal bodies, may it be well with your souls, and with mine, when the great shout and the sound of the shofar are heard! One American preacher from a previous generation, a man named Vance Havner when speaking of the end time, used to say: "I'm not looking for signs; I'm listening for a sound"! – the sound of the voice of the archangel, and of the shofar.

This blowing of the shofar at the time of the Rapture is arguably the most important sound of that instrument in all of time.

We may also be assured that it will be sudden. In I Cor.15:52 we are told that it will be

"… *in a moment, in the twinkling of an eye,* …"

It won't be a long, drawn-out, process. It will happen (as the late Tommy Cooper might have put it!) "just like that"!

The word translated "*caught up*" in I Thess.4:17, is from the Greek root *harpazo*. This has the idea of being snatched up. William Hendriksen has this to say: "The suddenness, the swiftness, and the divine power which is operative in this being snatched up are here emphasised. The survivors [saints] have been changed 'in a moment, in the twinkling of an eye' (I Cor.15:52)" (N.T.C. *in loc*).

Some may be aware of a period of time known as a "nano-second"! I use the expression "period of time" because I cannot think of anything more suitable. But a nano-second is one one-billionth of a second! That is, quite honestly, beyond my comprehension. It has been explained to me as the time it takes for light, travelling at just under 300,000 kms per second, to pass the width of a human hair! Mind-blowing! Yet I believe that if Paul had been privy to such information, he might well have written "... we shall all be changed in a nano-second."!

A number of years ago, the late David Wilkerson authored a "mock" newspaper – entitled "The Last News". In it, he imagined that the Rapture had taken place the night before. Here is part of the "lead story", under the headline:

"CHRIST RETURNS – Millions missing around the world"

"**At 12.05 a.m. today, a telephone operator reported three frantic calls regarding missing relatives. Within 15 minutes, all satellite, Internet, and other communications networks were jammed with similar inquiries.**

A spot check around the nation found the same situation in every city; sobbing husbands sought information about the mysterious disappearance of their wives. One husband reported, 'I turned on the light to ask my wife if she remembered to set the clock, but she was gone. Her bedclothes were there; her watch was on the floor – she just disappeared.'

An alarmed caller from Brooklyn tearfully reported, 'My husband just returned from the late shift ... I kissed him ... he just disappeared in my arms.'

Less than 35 minutes after the first calls were received, a well-known television executive took to the air with the first explanation of the mass midnight kidnapping. He asserted that the strange disappearance of millions last night was a Biblical prediction that suddenly exploded into fulfilment. In determined syllables he spelled out what he called the "rapture of the saints."

'Jesus Christ has returned to the earth and has taken His Christian people as His bride ... it has been forecast for centuries ... my own mother spoke often of this day. There is no hope. I have missed the only thing worth living for. I – like you – refused to believe in the literal coming of Jesus Christ.'" (see http://bibleprophecy-rapture.blogspot.co.uk/2009/05/end-times-rapture-newspaper.html).

The departure we shall make – certain, and sudden. However, we must also consider the destination we shall have.

> "... *we shall be caught up ... to meet the Lord in the air.*" (I Thess.4:17).

We won't depart merely in order to wander around, aimlessly, in space like rogue satellites, or even disembodied spirits! We will have a destination, a goal, to which we will go. And that destination will be the Christ Himself!

So there will be a Person we will meet. And we will meet Him "*in the air*".

Since the air was thought of, in Paul's contemporary culture, as being the abode of all manner of evil spirits; since the devil is even designated

"... *the prince of the power of the air,*" (Eph.2:2);

it is a measure of the complete supremacy of the Christ, that He should meet His people in that region.

So, although I would contend that these words be taken literally, they also have a symbolic meaning pointing, as they do, to the majesty and power of the victorious Jesus. He is the Person we shall meet.

But there is also a perfection we will gain. No matter how faithful a disciple of Jesus I might be, I am still, while dwelling in this mortal body, imperfect. There is, raging within me, that battle of which Paul wrote to the young church in Rome:

"*I cannot understand my own behaviour. I fail to carry out the things I want to do, and I find myself doing the very things I hate. When I act against my own will, that means I have a self that acknowledges that the Law is good, and so the thing behaving in that way is not my [converted] self but sin living in me.*" (7:15-127; Jerusalem Bible).

The devil continues to exert pressure on us; we are tainted by the influence of the world around us, from which we cannot really escape. Sanctification (see ch.14), the process of "perfecting" for the disciple of Jesus, is only completed when we enter the immediate presence of the Lord – either at our physical death, or at the Rapture. But then, we shall be perfect, even as He is perfect. (see I John 3:2).

So, at the Rapture, there is a departure that disciples of Jesus will make; there is a destination we will have; and there is a delight that we shall know.

> "... we, who are still living on the earth, will be swept up ... into the clouds to meet the Lord in the air. And, after that, we will be with Him for ever." (I Thess.4:17; J.B.Phillips).

Each of us, I am sure, knows the joy of being in the presence of a loved one. It may be a husband, or a wife; it may be a father, or a mother; it may be a brother, or a sister. It may well be that it is "just" a friend – someone who is as close to us as our dearest relatives. For me, that person is my wife. And words alone cannot express my feelings when I am with her – which is, I would contend, exactly as it should be! Sometimes, I think to myself: "Well, if I experience such an intense happiness when I am with my wife, what's it going to be like when I am "with the Lord" which, Paul assures us,

> "*is far better*" (Phil.1:23)"?!

And I find that I can't even begin to comprehend the intensity of that delight! "The principal happiness of heaven", writes Matthew Henry, "is this: "to be with the Lord", to see Him, live with Him, and enjoy Him for ever". (Commentary, I Thess., *in loc*).

But, as we think of the intensity with which we will behold Him, we must also rejoice in the eternity for which we will be with Him.

> "*we shall be with Him – for ever.*"

Not only do we have an intense delight in being with a loved one; we also, usually, hate to have to tear ourselves away, to be parted from, that loved one. We might even go as far as to say that we dread the very thought of separation – and, indeed, is not separation the main factor behind our natural grief on the physical death of one to whom we were at all close?! But this situation won't arise for the believer, when the Christ calls us to Himself. Because we are to be with Him for "the eternity of eternities".

Our feeble, finite, minds cannot even begin to grasp the vastness of eternity (but see ch.25!). Even "*for ever*" is too much for us. Yet this is the way it will be with Jesus. We will never be separated from Him, if we truly belong to Him, and He to us.

So Paul reaches the climax of this passage. "There are doubtless many points on which we should like further information; but when Paul come to that great fact, which includes everything else, and makes everything else unimportant, he ceases. There is nothing to add to it." (Leon Morris; I & II Thessalonians, p.89).

"*So we shall **always** be with the Lord.*" (*emphasis added*).

This is connected to the procedures in a Jewish wedding – which is somewhat different to a wedding in either France or Scotland! Permit me to talk you through the procedure, and how it is reflected in the union of the Lord Jesus and His church.

First of all, the father of the young man chooses a bride for his son. Paul writes to the disciples of Jesus in Ephesus and so, to us also:

> "*Blessed be the God and Father of our Lord Jesus Christ, Who has blessed us in Christ with every spiritual blessing in the heavenly places, even as **He chose us** in Him **before the foundation of the world**, that we should be holy and blameless before Him.*" (Eph 1:3-4).

If you are truly a disciple of Jesus, then you may rejoice that you have been chosen, by the Father, to be His bride.

Then when the young man made his proposal to the young woman chosen by his father, he did so by offering her a glass of wine. If she accepted the wine, she was accepting his proposal.

The next time that you participate in the Lord's Supper, and partake of the cup, remember that you have accepted the offer of Jesus, the Christ, to be His bride!

Having had his proposal of marriage accepted, the young man then returns to his father's house in order to prepare a room that he and his bride will use at the beginning of their marriage.

Speaking to the eleven – for Judas had already left to betray the Master – John records that Jesus said:

> "*In my Father's house are many rooms; if it were no so, would I have told you that I go to prepare a place for you?*" (John 14:2).

When the father is satisfied that the room is ready, he sends his son to claim his bride.

Jesus continues, in John 14:

> "*And when I go and prepare a place for you, I will come again and will take you to Myself, that where I am you may be also.*" (John 14:3).

The bride, during this time, wears a veil that signifies her betrothal. Of course, she longs for the day when she can remove that veil as a married woman. She doesn't know exactly when that will be – but she knows approximately, as it is usually about one year. To put it in Biblical terms regarding the Rapture, she knows the season, but not the day! Only the father of the bridegroom has that knowledge. Both Matthew, and Mark, record the statement of the Lord Jesus:

> "... *of that day or that hour no one knows, not even the angels in heaven, nor the Son, but **only the Father**.*" (Mark 13:32).

When the day comes, the groomsman/best man runs ahead of the groom, blowing the shofar, and shouting that the bridegroom is on his way. This usually happens at night time, so the bride must constantly be ready.

The written Word of God provides us with so many signs of the coming of the Bridegroom, - our Lord Jesus. Arguably the greatest of these is Israel, the nation, being reformed on May 14th, 1948 – the date on which, many are convinced, the prophetic clock started to tick!

As we look at the 'signs of the times', there can surely be no doubt in any Bible-believing person's mind, that we are in the very last days – that the Rapture is, to use an English-language idiom, "Just around the corner"!

Matthew records these interesting words of the Lord Jesus:

> *"... this gospel of the kingdom will be preached throughout the whole world, as a testimony to all nations; and then the end will come."* (Matt 24:14).

Some suggest that this means that the Rapture will not take place until the whole world has heard the Gospel. But that is not what Jesus is saying. He is saying that all nations will hear the Gospel message before the end, that is, His second advent.

You see, during the Tribulation, the Gospel will continue to be proclaimed by the two witnesses of Rev. 11:3. Who are these witnesses? We are not told, and attempts to identify them as individuals are, at best, speculation. Some have suggested that they are Moses and Elijah – representing the law and the prophets. This is often based on the record of the Mount of Transfiguration, when these two met, and talked with, the Lord Jesus. Others have suggested that they will be Joshua and Zerubbabel – based on the reference to olive trees, and lampstands in the book of the prophet Zechariah. But all that is revealed to us is that these two witnesses will prophesy for three and a half years – the first half of the Tribulation. During this time, I believe, many of the Children of Israel will come to recognise Yeshua as HaMashiach. The words of Jesus would suggest that there will be others who will realise their earlier error, and who will now recognise the Lord Jesus as Saviour, and Lord and King – but that is another message!

Now, I must make clear that there are those believe that the Rapture will take place half-way through the Great Tribulation; some who believe that it will take place at the end; and, of course, some who do not believe that there will be a Rapture. So why do I believe that the Rapture of the true disciples of Jesus will take place, and will do so before the Great Tribulation?

The final words of Paul in our passage from the first letter to the believers in Thessalonica are:

> "*Therefore comfort one another with these words.*"

This is just one reason why I believe, firmly, that the Rapture will take place <u>before</u> the Tribulation. I am unable to see any comfort in the thought of having to go through that final period of earth's history!

And then just a little further in, Paul encourages these dear people with these words:

> "*For God has not destined us for wrath, but to obtain salvation through our Lord Jesus Christ, Who died for us so that whether we wake or sleep we might live with Him. Therefore encourage one another and build one another up, just as you are doing.*" (I Thess. 5:9-11).

If I am "not destined for wrath" then I cannot see how I would have to go through the Tribulation!

It's exciting to think of the Rapture of the Church. To think of the departure we shall make – the certainty of it, and the suddenness of it. To think of the destination we shall have – the Person we will meet, and the perfection we will gain. To think of the delight that we shall know – in the intensity with which we will behold Him, and the eternity for which we will be with Him.

This is the Rapture.

I want to leave you with just three questions;

1 Have you been washed – in the blood of the Lord Jesus?

2 Are you watching – for His 'coming in the clouds'?

3 Are you waiting -?

When that great shout is heard; when the sound of the shofar echoes throughout the world; may you and I be among those who are snatched up, in a nanosecond, to be forever with the Lord.

Chapter 21

CHURCH

> "An army of ordinary people
> A kingdom where love is the key
> A city, a light to the nations
> Heirs to the promise are we
> A people whose life is in Jesus
> A nation together we stand
> Only through grace are we worthy
> Inheritors of the land."
> (Dave Bilbrough)

During pre-membership classes in a Fellowship in which I was involved in leadership, I often heard a friend make this statement: "You can be in the church, but not in the Kingdom; but you can't be in the Kingdom without wanting to be in the church" (*Tom Nelson*). The Kingdom to which he referred was, of course, the Kingdom of God/Heaven. But what is the Church?

To many, it is the building in which people pray, and worship God; the place in which one might be married; the possible locus for a funeral service. This, of course, is totally wrong. The church is not the building, but the people who gather there in the Name of Jesus. I love the notice-board that I saw, many years ago, outside a building in the city of Edinburgh: "This is the meeting-place of [*Name*] Church!"

We'd been teaching colleagues for almost twenty years, but we'd never had what might be called a serious conversation. That was at least partly, due to the fact that, in both the former school building, and in the most recently-opened one, we were as far apart physically, as it was possible to be.

But I'd been helping out in a particular congregation, and had got to know some of the members quite well. One day, I asked if anyone knew this particular colleague, as she had lived in the area for, as far as I knew, her whole life. One of the men in the room immediately informed me that she was his niece.

Some time later, I discovered that the uncle had been in hospital and so I made a point of going over to my colleague to ask how he was. The news was good, and I was ready to move on. However she seemed to want to continue the conversation and, as it progressed she came out with an unexpected comment. "I've not been to church for a long time. I used to be a good worker in the church, but I've given up on it." And then, very quickly, she added, "But although I've given up on the church, I've never given up on God."

"I've given up on the church, but I've never given up on God." was reminded of words written over 50 years ago, in a book entitled *Christian Faith Today* (S.C.Neill). "Nothing in the contemporary scene is more striking than the general regard which is felt for Jesus Christ, and the general dislike of the organised church which bears His name." And it was the theologian, Søren Kierkegaard, who once wrote that "Whereas Christ turned water into wine, the church has succeeded in doing something more difficult: it has turned wine into water"!! My former colleague's statement raises a very interesting question – "What is the church?"

Thankfully, the New Testament gives us a number of pictures that may help.

First of all, the Word of God says that the church is the flock of God. The picture of the people of God as a flock is, of course, common in both the Old, and the New, Testaments. I suspect that the one part of the OT that many people, even today, might be able to quote is, not the Ten Commandments, but the 23rd Psalm

> "*YHWH is my …… Shepherd.*"

The prophet Isaiah painted a similar word-picture. Speaking of YHWH, he writes:

> "*He will feed His flock like a shepherd. He will carry the lambs in His arms, holding them close to His heart. He will gently lead the mother sheep with their young.*" (40:11).

In the New Testament, we find the Lord Jesus referring to Himself as

> "*the good Shepherd*"

Who gives His life for His sheep; and Who knows His sheep individually, and intimately. (Jn.10:11,14). And in Peter's First Letter, we find him speaking to those who are elders in the church and exhorting them to

> "*Care for the flock that God has entrusted to you*" (5:2; NLT)

– i.e. the individual fellowship of God's people that they are serving. And he writes of

> "*… the head Shepherd …*" (5:4; TLB)

– even Jesus.

So what does this picture tell us about the church? Well, sheep tend to flock together – so we might say that the church is people who come together. Sheep are also very foolish animals that depend totally on the shepherd to care for them and provide for them – so, as church, we are totally dependent upon Jesus, our head Shepherd to guide us and guard us; to provide and protect us. Sheep are very useful animals. Jewish shepherds tended their sheep, not for meat – which would have been a one-off provision – but for wool, and milk, and lambs. The people of God should be useful to the Lord – reproducing, as others are brought to a saving knowledge of the Master, through our work and witness. Sheep were used for sacrifice – and we are called to be

"... *living sacrifices*...",

doing the will of Father God (Rom.12:1-2).

The church, as the flock of God, is dependent upon Him for nutrition, for safety, for guidance. It is under His control; He has complete authority over it. But the church is also composed of individuals. So the question must be "Is all of that true of me?!" Am I prepared to let it be true? Totally dependent upon God; totally subject to God.

A second, Biblical, description of the church is as the household of faith. In Gal.6:10 Paul writes

"*So then, as we have opportunity, let us do good to all men, and especially to those who are of the household of faith.*", or "*our family in the faith*"

as the Good News Bible translation has it.

What a lovely picture of the church that should be – a household, a family, all pulling together towards the same goals. A picture of shared love; of shared values; of mutual respect.

And, sadly, how different from the picture that we see of so much of the church today! The church should be the company of people among whom, more than anywhere else, others should be helped, and encouraged, and built up.

Sharing the blessings we receive involves doing good to all men. There are those who do evil (Ps.34:16); there are those who actually return evil for good (Ps.35:12). The vast majority, I suspect, tend to return good for good, and evil for evil (I Thess.5:15, Lk.6:32-35). But the Christian, the one who is truly a member of the flock of God, of the household of faith, is supposed to return good for evil! We are to

> "*do good to all men*".

You see, it is not just by what we say that we witness to the world, it is also by our actions. My wife and I have – at this date! – only once visited the beautiful Italian town of Perugia. And across the valley we were able to see the much-better-known village of Assisi. And it was Francis of Assisi who is famously reported (although there is some doubt!) as having remarked: "Preach the Gospel at all times and, when necessary, use words."!

But as we do good to all men, we must give priority to the family of God, the household of faith, the fellowship of believers. This is not to suggest that the church should ever be some sort of exclusive clique. The church will not grow unless we welcome the unchurched.

But it's a matter of balance. Certainly the believers in Paul's day would have many more needs since many of them suffered, physically, mentally, emotionally, for their faith. That's why I encourage fellowships and congregations, when I'm privileged to share with them, to remember the persecuted church in over 50 countries around the world. And I hope that many, who have access to internet facilities, will check out my premier blog site (www.crazyrev.blogspot.com), go to the bottom of the page, and use the links there for, for example, **Christian Solidarity Worldwide – Voice for the Voiceless;** or **Release International - The voice of the persecuted church** (to which ministry, all royalties from the sale of my books go, directly!). The dear folk, some of whose stories may be read on these, and similar, websites, and who suffer unspeakable privation and persecution for the sake of the Lord Jesus, are members of the household of faith.

Yet again, we find that, in the pages of the New Testament, the church is described as God's building. Writing to the early fellowship of believers in Corinth, Paul had this to say:

> *"We work together as partners who belong to God. You are God's field, God's building – not ours."* (I Cor.3:9).

And we note, in passing, that the church is also God's field, and that believers are to be partners – with one another, and with Father God.

Just a couple of years before I retired from the teaching profession, my school moved into a new, hi-tech, 21st century, state-of-the-art, school building. Well, that was the theory! The reality was that we left a building that, had it not been deliberately allowed to deteriorate over the last few years of its life was, in many ways, far superior to that into which we had moved. The new building appeared, to many of us, to have been thrown up, with no apparent concern for quality and strength. A bad plan, in my opinion, poorly executed!

Father God is concerned that His church is a quality building. And that means meeting certain conditions. It must be built on the right foundation – that one foundation of which we sometimes sing – the foundation that is the Lord Jesus Himself. Not on a personality; not on some particular methodology; not on specific doctrines; but on the Master.

It must be built with the right materials. Paul speaks of gold, silver, and precious stones, rather than wood, hay, or stubble (I Cor.3:12). Some suggest that he is giving, here, a picture of the different kinds of people who may be found within a church setting; but is it not more likely that he is speaking about the wisdom of God, as it is found in His written Word? The Corinthians, it would appear, were attempting to build the church by man's wisdom – the wisdom of the world – when they should have been depending on the wisdom of God, as found in the Word!

The right foundation; the right materials; and the right plan. I've known congregations, and fellowships, and other Christian organisations, that are run as businesses rather than as part of the Biblical church! I have occasionally, in the past, inquired about a pastoral vacancy – and received an Application Form that made it look as if I would be applying for a position as CEO in some multi-national company! So much for seeking God's man, and then issuing a call! The world runs on promotion, prestige, the power of money, people who are seen to be 'important'. But the true church of God depends on prayer, on the power of God the Holy Spirit, on such unworldly concepts as humility, sacrifice, service. The church that merely emulates the world may appear to have a measure of success – but I have seen, all too often, such organisations crumble to dust. The church of which I read in the Acts of the Apostles had none of the trappings of 21st century success. They owned no property; they had no direct influence on the government; they had no large treasury; their leaders were, in the main, uneducated men; they brought in no big-name celebrities. Yet that was a church of which it was said that they had

"*turned the world upside-down*". (Acts 17:6).

And the church must be built with the right motive – the glory of Almighty God. Those Corinthian believers were glorifying men – arguing about whether they were Paulites, or Apollo-ites, or Cephas-ites, and were dividing the church by their carnal activity. Had they been seeking to glorify the Lord, there would have been unity and harmony in their gatherings.

It's interesting, is it not, that Jesus' great High Priestly prayer, as recorded in John 17 – the true "Lord's Prayer", by the way! – was that His disciples, both then and now, might be one! And the evidence, He said, that would convince the world that we are His disciples is that we love one another.

The flock of God; the household of faith; God's building; and the church is also referred to as the Bride of Christ. Here, surely, is one of the most beautiful descriptions of the church. Writing, again to the Corinthian church, Paul has this to say:

> *"I feel a divine jealousy for you, for I betrothed you to Christ to present you as a pure bride to her one Husband."* (II Cor.11:2).

The apostle gives, here, a picture of a particular relationship – one that is personal; willing; intimate. I like to think that I have a reasonably good relationship with the vast majority of the people I know. That relationship, I am happy to be able to say, is particularly close with my daughters, both of whom I love dearly and whose love for their dad I have never doubted. But my deepest human relationship is with my wife. It is she who has put up with me, even in the light of the faults and failings that only she, and the Lord, know for, now, over forty years.

Sadly, we now live in a culture and society in which the Biblical concept of marriage, as ordained by Almighty God, has been steadily eroded, and devalued, over the last number of decades.

But the picture that Paul paints with these words "... is that of a loving father who has a daughter engaged to be married. He feels it his privilege and duty to keep her pure, so that he can present her to her (bridegroom) with joy and not with sorrow." (Warren Wiersbe, *Be Encouraged*).

A virgin bride. That is what the church – and that means every individual believer – is called to be. The danger, then, is one of unfaithfulness. The engaged young woman owes her love and allegiance to one, and one alone – her fiancé. If she shares herself with any other man, she is guilty of infidelity. So, as believers, when we allow anything, or anyone, else to come between us and the Lord, we are being unfaithful to Him. "A divided heart", writes Warren Wiersbe, "leads to a defiled life, and a destroyed relationship." (*op cit*). And that is true in both the area of physical, and spiritual, relationships.

The flock of God; the household of faith; God's building; the Bride of Christ; and, finally, the Body of Christ. This final picture is one of maximum intimacy. The Lord Jesus is the Head, the church is the Body. But this picture refers not only to the relationship between the church and her Head, but to the relationship between the members of the church.

All of us are familiar with our own bodies. If my leg is sore, other parts of my body suffer – either by suffering themselves, or by having to work harder to make up for the injured member.

And, of course, all the parts of my body are different, and each needs the other. If a giant nose were to slither up into the pulpit one Sunday during the worship service, it would be a very unusual situation – but it wouldn't be very effective!

Listen to Paul as he writes, again to the early church in Corinth:

> *"For just as the body is one and has many members, and all the members of the body, though many, are one body, so it is with Christ. For by one Spirit we were all baptized into one body – Jews or Greeks, slaves or free – and all were made to drink of one Spirit.*
>
> *"For the body does not consist of one member but of many. If the foot should say, 'Because I am not a hand, I do not belong to the body,' that would not make it any less a part of the body. And if the ear should say, 'Because I am not an eye, I do not belong to the body,' that would not make it any less a part of the body. If the whole body were an eye, where would be the hearing? If the whole body were an ear, where would be the sense of smell? But as it is, God arranged the organs in the body, each one of them, as he chose. If all were a single organ, where would the body be? As it is, there are many parts, yet one body. The eye cannot say to the hand, 'I have no need of you,' nor again the head to the feet, 'I have no need of you.'"* (I Cor.12:12-21).

Spiritual gifts are tools with which to build up the church. They are not toys with which to play; nor are they weapons with which to fight. "My gift is more important than your gift" is **not** the way in which the church exhibits itself as the body of Christ.

Rob James has written: "I will always be grateful that I stumbled across a copy of *Cinderella's Betrothal Gifts* by Michael Griffiths. Griffiths reminded me that 'charismata' derives from the Greek word for 'grace' and, because of this, we would do best to think of spiritual gifts as 'serving grace'.

In other words, spiritual gifts should be seen as God's grace poured out on a congregation in such a way that it allows His people to do His work. Such a view of spiritual gifts helps us avoid the danger of treating them as some kind of personal trophy, or certificate of merit.

Gifts, then, are not so much possessed as exercised; and only exercised properly when they are a means of blessing other people." (Rob James; *Inspire* magazine, CPO, Worthing, June 2011)

And it's that sort of picture of the church as the body of Christ that encourages me to be involved with my brothers and sisters in Christ – those members of the body that I may never meet in this life, but who are one with me in Him – who suffer in ways that I am unable to fully comprehend, for the sake of the Gospel.

Christian fellowship – being part of the body of Christ – is much more than a pat on the back and a handshake. It is more than a coming together once a week, and having no form of meaningful communication from one Sunday worship service to the next. It is a willingness to share the burdens, and the blessings, of others so that all of us may grow together, and bring glory to the Lord.

The church – not just a particular congregation, fellowship, or denomination – but those who are

> "*all one in Christ Jesus.*" (Gal.3:28).

There are other pictures in the pages of God's Word. But let these five thumbnail sketches suffice. It's:

The flock of God – may each one of us follow the Good Shepherd;

The household of faith – let us be certain that we have made that conscious decision of placing our trust in the saving work of the Lord Jesus at Calvary;

God's building – the very temple of God the Holy Spirit. May we truly be living stones;

The bride of Christ – let us be ever watchful, looking expectantly for the coming of the Bridegroom as King of kings, and Lord of lords;

The Body of Christ – every member participating with others in that love that comes only from the Father; functioning in a healthy, harmonious, way; treating others as more important than ourselves; sharing not only the joys, but also the sorrows, the pain, and the persecution of those parts of the body who bear, in their mortal bodies, the very marks of the Lord Jesus.

When disciples of Jesus live like that, we might be a church that is truly worthy of the name – and we will give all of the praise and the glory to our glorious Head. Hallelujah!

Chapter 22

The Trinity

"Holy, holy, holy; merciful and mighty –
God in three Persons, blesséd Trinity"
(Reginald Beber)

When I attended my Grammar School, many years ago now, one of my best subjects was mathematics – and I was particularly good at arithmetic. So I know that three times one equals three. And I know that if I have one apple in each hand, and one held in my mouth, I have three apples. And, indeed, one doesn't have to be a mathematical expert to work that out. And that is why the Christian doctrine of the Trinity is such a major problem for so many – even some of those within the ranks of the clergy! According to Augustine, the 4th century theologian, "If you deny the Trinity, you lose your soul; if you try to explain the Trinity, you shall lose your mind." But, in this chapter, it's the great word of the Christian faith at which I'd like us to look.

It's an integral part of every major creed, or statement of belief, in the history of the Christian Church. Yet it's a doctrine, or teaching, that has caused great confusion, and great consternation. The first thing that we have to emphasise is that we are not at liberty to assume that God must be like a human being. Listen to these words spoken through the prophet Isaiah:

"To whom can you compare God? What image can you find to resemble Him?" (40:18); *"To whom will you compare Me? Who is my equal? ... I alone am God! I am God, and there is none like Me!"* (46:5, 9).

So, just because I may be unable to conceive of one Being, being three Beings, merely shows how little I know and understand! The late Rev George B. Duncan, used to point out that **if** he could understand everything **about** God – then he would **be** God! The created cannot even hope to begin to fully understand the Creator.

But, of course, there's much more to it than that! To stop there would be seen by many sceptical people as a bit of a cop-out! So let's see what happens if we approach the subject from a scientific point of view. A scientific theory is, for the most part, a reasoned explanation of phenomena that have been observed. And the doctrine of the Trinity is a reasoned explanation of what we observe to be the phenomena of God, in the Bible. As members of certain of the cults would quickly point out, the word, itself, is not to be found anywhere in the pages of the Bible. But, as I hope to demonstrate, the doctrine is clearly taught. The word is just a convenient term employed by theologians and the like to describe these phenomena. The early church, through its councils and the study by its deepest thinkers, was so overwhelmed by the vast amount of evidence for the doctrine of the Trinity, that it has been universally accepted as one of the points that decide whether, or not, one is a Christian in a fully Biblical sense.

Whilst I was at University, I had to study Logic. And that discipline works on premises that lead to a conclusion. Here, our first premise is that the Bible clearly teaches that there is only one God. The second premise is the Bible clearly teaches that there are three distinct Persons called God, and Whom we know as the Father, the Son, and the Holy Spirit. So, we are led to the conclusion that these three Persons – Father, Son, and Holy Spirit, are the one God. We're going to look at some of the evidence for all of this, from the Bible, and then try to put it all together with some linguistics to help us out. Now don't worry – I won't try to baffle you with a load of heavy theology! Rather, I'll try to follow the example of Him Who said

> "*Come to Me, all who labour and are heavy laden, and I will give you rest. Take My yoke upon you, and learn from Me; for I am gentle and lowly in heart, and you will find rest for your souls. For My yoke is easy, and My burden is light.*" (Matt.11:28-30).

Our first premise was that there is only one God.

This premise is almost universally accepted by those who claim to be Christian, and so one clear statement should be sufficient to make the point. Writing, near to the end of his own earthly life, to his young friend, Timothy, the apostle Paul states

> "*For there is one God, and there is one Mediator between God and men, the Man Christ Jesus, who gave Himself as a ransom for all, the testimony to which was borne at the proper time.*" (I Tim.2:5-7).

> "*For there is one God.*"

Our second premise requires marginally more time, and thought. It was, you remember, that there are three Persons who are referred to as God.

The first of these is God the Father. That there is a Person named the Father, Who is called God, is acknowledged in a host of Biblical verses. In I Cor.1:3 we read,

"Grace to you and peace from God our Father and the Lord Jesus Christ."

An identical form of words is used in Phil.1:2; and in Rom.1:7 and, lest those with some Biblical knowledge come to the conclusion that it was only Paul who held to the deity of the Father, Peter, in his first letter, and in the first 21 verses, makes the same point clear. Not even the cultists seek to deny this point.

But what about the Son? Well, the Bible certainly seems to make clear that Jesus of Nazareth is also God. Listen to these opening words from John's account of the Gospel:

> *"In the beginning was the Word, and the Word was with God, and the Word was God. He was in the beginning with God; all things were made through Him, and without Him was not anything made that was made. ... He came to His own home, and His own people received Him not. But to all who received Him, who believed in His name, He gave power to become children of God; ... And the Word became flesh and dwelt among us, full of grace and truth; we have beheld His glory, glory as of the only Son from the Father. ... No one has ever seen God; the only Son, who is in the bosom of the Father, He has made Him known."* (1:1-18).

I would suggest that, even at one hearing, those words make absolutely clear that the Word is God; that the Word became flesh in the One we know as Jesus of Nazareth; and that the Word was the Son. Putting all of that together, we are forced to the conclusion that Jesus of Nazareth was God the Son, in human flesh – what theologians refer to as the Incarnation.

Elsewhere, Paul says, concerning this same Jesus, that

"... *in Him the whole fullness of Deity*..." (what could be clearer?) "... *dwells bodily, and you have come to fullness of life in Him, Who is the Head of all rule and authority.*" (Col.2:9-10).

To Whom else could that apply other than Almighty God?

Now, of course, I've been around long enough to have been challenged by some of those cultists who deny the Deity of the Lord Jesus, yet who claim to accept the Bible. They will claim that Jesus didn't know everything, therefore wasn't omniscient, therefore wasn't God. They will claim that He is referred to as the firstborn, indicating that He was just one of many. Most, if not all, of their argument is based on a total misunderstanding of the nature of the Incarnation, and on ignorance of the contemporary culture. When God became Man as Jesus, the Christ He didn't give up His divine attributes, or characteristics. He simply took on a human nature, and denied His human mind access to His divine mind. To have done otherwise would have negated the whole concept of the Incarnation! Likewise, when He is referred to as the firstborn in e.g., Rom.8; Rev.1, this has nothing to do with a chronological sequence, but refers to His position over all others: to His pre-eminence.

That leaves the Holy Spirit. Is there any evidence to support this claim that He, too, is God in every sense?

Some who are willing to accept that the Father is God, and even that the Son may have divine characteristics, have great difficulty in accepting the deity of the Holy Spirit. Some don't even attribute personality to Him, preferring to speak of Him as a force of some sort or another. But the Bible is perfectly clear. The Holy Spirit is a Person, and He is God. Listen to these words. Jesus is speaking to the disciples about His impending return to the glory of the Father's Presence.

> "...*I tell you the truth: It is for your good that I am going away. Unless I go away, the Counsellor will not come to you; but if I go, I will send Him to you*. ... "*I have much more to say to you, more than you can now bear. But when He, the Spirit of truth, comes, He will guide you into all truth. He will not speak on His own; He will speak only what He hears, and He will tell you what is yet to co*me." (John 16:7-13; NIV).

Did you notice all of those personal pronouns, referring to the Holy Spirit?

But not only is personality attributed to the Holy Spirit; deity is clearly attributed as well. Let one example suffice. In Acts 5:3-4 we read

> "*But Peter said, 'Ananias, why has Satan filled your heart to lie to the Holy Spirit and to keep back part of the proceeds of the land? While it remained unsold, did it not remain your own? And after it was sold, was it not at your disposal? How is it that you have contrived this deed in your heart? You have not lied to men but to God.*'"

Peter is equating a lie to the Holy Spirit with lying to God. In other words, to lie to the Holy Spirit is to lie to God. And, since one cannot lie to an impersonal force, this passage further teaches the personality of the Holy Spirit.

So to come back to our earlier conclusion: the three Persons are one God. I want to look at one final passage of the many that could be referred to, that shows this great doctrine of the Triune God. In what is often referred to as the Great Commission, Jesus instructs His disciples to

"Go therefore and make disciples of all nations, baptizing them in the Name of the Father and of the Son and of the Holy Spirit, ..." (Matt 28:19).

Now, it's important to realise that the Greek word *onoma*, which is translated as "Name" is a singular word. The one Name covers all three Persons. And the union of these three Persons in the form of baptism proves that the Son and Holy Spirit are equal with the Father. Nothing would be more absurd or, indeed, blasphemous than to unite the name of a creature – be it a man or an angel – with the name of the ever-living God in this solemn rite. If Jesus was a mere man or an angel, as is held by many who deny His divinity, and if the Holy Spirit was a mere force, an "attribute" of God, then it would have been the height of absurdity to use a form like this, or to direct the apostles to baptise people in these terms.

Over the centuries, different people have tried to illustrate the doctrine in different ways.

The way that I have found to be most helpful is to use myself as an illustration! Imagine that we are together, in the same room, and two young ladies enter. If you were to point to me, and ask them "Who is that?" then although they would be highly unlikely to use the exact terminology, it would be perfectly proper for them to answer "That is father". They, of course, would be my daughters. Imagine then, that an elderly couple arrive and that you ask them the same question. In their case, a perfectly acceptable answer would be "That is son", for they would have been my late parents. The door opens a third time, and a lady walks in, alone. Her answer to your question is "That is husband", for she is my dear wife.

So, you have been given three answers to the same question, and each of them applies to me. But I am only one individual! Yet I am father, son, and husband. And, indeed, I could bring many other people into the room and you would discover that this one individual – me – is also brother, nephew, cousin, uncle, neighbour, teacher, friend, preacher, colleague, and so on, and so on, and so on. Indeed, if I may say this with all reverence, I am so many different people, that God being Three seems to be pretty tame by comparison!

And, of course, I was (and am) at all times, the one complete being. When I visited my parents, I did not leave my own fatherhood behind. When my wife and I went out together, I did not cease to be a son. When playing with my children, I was still a husband.

The problem is one of language. When we say "person" we think "individual". However, the root of the word is the Latin *persona* and that was the mask that was worn by actors in the Roman and Greek theatre. I might appear on the stage and be met with booing and hissing. This was because I was holding in front of my face the mask, the *persona*, of the villain of the play. A little later I might reappear on stage to be greeted with cheering and rapturous applause. This time, I would be carrying in front of my face the mask, the *persona*, of the hero. Same me, different *personae* (the plural of *persona*).

Now, of course, that is no more than an analogy – and no analogy is perfect. However, while what I have shared is, itself, open to certain criticism, it is my hope that it helps to, at least, make clear that one being may have a number of different personae.

We find the same concept in the Hebrew language. In Genesis 1:26-27 we read:

> "Then God said, 'Let Us make man in Our image, after Our likeness; and let them have dominion over the fish of the sea, and over the birds of the air, and over the cattle and over all the earth, and over every creeping thing that creeps upon the earth.' So God created man in His own

image, in the image of God He created him; male and female He created them."

Notice, if you will, the apparently haphazard combination of singular and plural words! Almighty God refers to Himself in both the singular and in the plural; and He refers to humankind in the same way. This is because, in Hebrew, the plural does not refer simply to numbers. It refers to different 'kinds'. So God is One – but is also plural in kind. The different Personae are not identical. The same applies to humankind. One humanity, but a plurality of kinds – male and female.

Using the English language, we discover that there, too, singular and plural may merge. When a team (singular!) plays a game of whatever sport, it is one team – but it is comprised of a plurality of players, each of whom is different from the others. We often speak about "the government", as if it is a singular entity. Yet we know that it is comprised of a plurality of Ministers of State, supported by a vast number of Civil Servants. Many of those who read a book like this will be members of a congregation! A single congregation; a plurality of members.

Even in the realm of mathematics, things are not as illogical as they might, at first, seem! If I add three ones together – 1+1+1 – I do, indeed, get the answer 3. However, if I multiply three ones together – 1x1x1 – I get, that's right, 1! It's all a matter of relationship.

Every redeemed individual, is reconciled with God the Father, through the sacrificial death of God the Son, and brought into newness of life by God the Holy Spirit. It is this doctrine of the Trinity that underlies and gives significance and consistency to the teaching of the Scriptures as to the processes of salvation. Without the doctrine of the Trinity, the conscious Christian life would be thrown into confusion and left in disorganization if not, indeed, given an air of unreality. With the doctrine of the Trinity, order, significance and reality are brought to every element of it. Accordingly, the doctrine of the Trinity and the doctrine of redemption, historically, stand or fall together.

Understanding even something of the doctrine of the Trinity may be useful. But that doesn't bring salvation. It is when you turn to the Triune God, confessing your own sinfulness; repenting of your sins, and accepting His wonderful offer of new life; that you become one of the redeemed. Have you taken that step of commitment to God – Father, Son, and Holy Spirit? If not, permit me to encourage you, indeed urge you, to do something about it, while you have time.

Chapter 23

JESUS

*"There is a Name I love to hear; I love to speak its worth.
It sounds like music in my ear – the sweetest name on earth."*
(F.Whitfield)

As we approach the end of this book, we come to a word that is inestimably more than a word. We come to the word that is the most important in the whole of the written Word of God. We come to a word that is a Name; a Name that is above every name; the Name of Jesus.

The Name itself means 'Saviour' and, in its Hebrew form of *Yeshu'a*, was not uncommon among the Jewish people who lived 2,000 years ago, many of whom called their sons after the great leader, Joshua – either in memory of him or, even more likely in a culture in which a name was much more than a means of personal identification, and more an indication of one's character, in the hope that the son thus named would grow up to be a great leader of his people – perhaps even the promised Messiah who would free his people from foreign subjugation!

In looking at that Name, it is not my intention to produce a word study upon it. Rather, I want to ask some questions about the One with Whom it has been especially connected for more than 2,000 years – Jesus of Nazareth.

The first question has to do with His historical existence. Are you convinced about Him? Few, if any, of those who would normally be reading a book such as this would doubt the historical fact of the existence of a man named Jesus of Nazareth, Who lived in the Roman province of Judaea, some 2,000 years ago. Attempts that have been made to disprove his existence during the past couple of hundred years have all failed. In the early centuries A.D., not even the bitterest enemies of Christianity had any thought of denying that Jesus lived, and died, in Judaea, and that He performed wonderful works – however they might have attributed the power by which He performed them. Nor, at the present time, does any objective historian deny the historical fact of Jesus. Indeed, His life, and death, and resurrection must be reckoned among the best-established facts of history.

But, of course, there was much more to Jesus than just a physical existence at a particular point in past time. For there were claims that He made, and there were claims made about Him which, if we are to think seriously about Him at all, must be given careful consideration. To look at all of them would be a book in itself, but let's take a few examples.

He claimed to be able to forgive sin – and not just individual wrongdoings, but all sin! That was His word to, for example, the paralytic brought to Jesus by four friends.

> *"When Jesus returned to Capernaum several days later, the news spread quickly that He was back home. Soon the house where He was staying was so packed with visitors that there was no more room, even outside the door. While He was preaching God's word to them, four men arrived carrying a paralysed man on a mat. They couldn't bring him to Jesus because of the crowd, so they dug a hole through the roof above his head. Then they lowered the*

man on his mat, right down in front of Jesus. Seeing their faith, Jesus said to the paralysed man, 'My child, your sins are forgiven.'

But some of the teachers of religious law who were sitting there thought to themselves, 'What is He saying? This is blasphemy! Only God can forgive sins!'" (Mark 2:1-7; NLT).

He claimed to be life itself. Someone has written, concerning Him: "He did not say He knew the way, the truth, and the life; nor that He taught them. He did not make Himself the exponent of a new system; **He declared Himself to be the final key to all mysteries.**"

He claimed to be the Light of the world – the One by Whom all things are seen more clearly. He claimed to be the First and the Last; the Alpha and the Omega. He claimed to be the Everlasting and Eternal One.

He is spoken of as Lord, and as Saviour. He accepts the worship and adoration of men as His due. He raises the dead.

All of this, and every other claim, may be summed up in just one claim – Jesus is God, YHWH, the Creator and Sustainer of the Universe; in human form; equal with the Father. Indeed, this was the charge laid against Him and that led to His crucifixion:

> *"When Jesus came out wearing the crown of thorns and the purple robe, Pilate said to them, 'Here is the man!' As soon as the chief priests and their officials saw Him, they shouted, 'Crucify! Crucify!' But Pilate answered, 'You take Him and crucify Him. As for me, I find no basis for a charge against Him.' The Jews insisted, 'We have a law, and according to that law He must die, because **He***

claimed to be the Son of God.'" (John 19:5-7; NIV *emphasis added*).

He was, as far as the contemporary Jewish leadership was concerned, a blasphemer. John records an incident in which Jesus made the statement:

> "*'The Father and I are One.' Once again the people picked up stones to kill Him. Jesus said, 'At my Father's direction I have done many good works. For which one are you going to stone me?' They replied, 'We're stoning you not for any good work, but for blasphemy! You, a mere man,* **claim to be God.**"* (10:30-33; NLT; *emphasis added*)

What a stupendous claim! And, if it is true, it should have a profound effect upon our lives. Believing, born-again, disciples of Jesus are convinced that it is true. Are you? Are you convinced about Him – not only the historical fact of His existence, but also the claims made by Him, and made about Him?

The second question we must ask, follows on from the first. If you are convinced about Him, are you also conscious of Him? Are you aware of the reality of His presence? He is alive – but is He alive to you?!

It is perfectly possible for me to be convinced of, for example, the prowess of a particular sports personality, or athlete. I may be told that so-and-so claims to be able to run a mile in 3 mins 45 secs. may see evidence of that ability to do so on film, or through television. And I may thus become utterly convinced that the claim is valid and true. But I am not conscious of that person! He, or she, is but a distant figure with whom I have no relationship at all let alone a vital relationship!

And it can be the same with Jesus. I can be convinced about Him – and stop there. I can believe all that I have learned about Him – and go no further. I can accept the validity of every claim that He made – and not allow Him to have the slightest effect on my life.

But the disciple of Jesus; the one who has entered into a saving relationship with Him; the one who acknowledges Him as Saviour and Lord; is not only convinced about Him, but is also conscious of Him. Why should this be? Simply because of the bond of love that exists between them.

Have you ever had the experience of being somewhere, and suddenly being conscious that someone whom you love has arrived? You haven't seen the person, but the bond of love between you has, as it were, triggered this awareness of the other's presence.

Jesus, speaking to His early disciples, said:

> "*He who has my commandments and keeps them, he it is who loves Me; and he who loves Me will be loved by My Father, and I will love him and manifest Myself to him.*"
> (John 14:21).

What He is saying there – to His disciples today just as much as to those who heard His very words – is that if I am obedient to Him, then that is a sign of my love for Him; and that if I thus love Him, then He will make Himself real to me – I will be conscious of Him.

In the first prayer in the marriage service that I used to conduct, were these words concerning the couple who were standing before me: "May they be as conscious of Your presence as they are of each other's, and so enter into marriage as in Your sight." And that was a totally sincere prayer. For I believed then, as I believe now, that only with God's presence in a home, and in a marriage, is there any guarantee of real happiness and joy. And the wonderful thing is that, if the two persons concerned have been born again by the power of God the Holy Spirit, then they will be conscious of Jesus – as Saviour, and Lord, and Friend.

But what about you? Are you conscious of Him because of the bond of love that exists between you? Can you talk with Him as you would a human friend?

The final question asks if you are committed to Him. It's a logical conclusion! If I am convinced about Him – about all of His claims, and the claims made about Him – then I cannot do other than love Him. And if I love Him, and am obedient to Him, I will be conscious of His presence. And if I am convinced about Him, and am conscious of Him, then what else can I do but commit myself to Him? And this means handing over everything to His control, absolutely and completely. It means putting Him first in every aspect of life. It means seeking His will, His guidance, about everything – in my choice of a career, a place to live, a husband or wife (or, indeed, of remaining single, for that is His will for many). It means going where He would have me go; doing what He would have me do. It means being able to say, with Paul,

> "*For me to live is Christ, and to die is gain*" (Phil.1:21)

– and mean it! It means being able to say that

> "*... it is no longer I who live, but Christ Who lives in me*" (Gal.2:20).

It means saying with John the Baptiser, concerning Jesus, that

> "*He must increase, but I must decrease*" (John 3:30).

And it means worshipping Him at every opportunity, and in everything that I do; witnessing to Him, not only by what I say, but by the very quality of my life.

Of course, that is no soft option! The life of the true disciple of Jesus is one of the most difficult and demanding that there is - just take some time to research the persecuted church in some fifty countries world-wide! - and each one of us fails Him miserably at times. But it's the most worthwhile life too; and the most exciting.

"How sweet the Name of Jesus sounds, in a believer's ear", wrote the hymn-writer.

The old chorus went:

"Jesus, Jesus, Jesus; sweetest name I know.
Fills my every longing; keeps me singing as I go."

Jesus. Not merely a great word of the Christian faith, but the name that is above every name.

Are you convinced about Him?

Are you conscious of Him?

Are you committed to Him?

If you are, then you know just how wonderful He is. If you're not, then you're missing out on so much.

If you are, then He is a reality – a daily, living experience. If you're not then Jesus is, indeed, just a word.

If you are, then rejoice in His companionship, His love, His daily outpouring of grace. If you're not, then resolve to do something positive about it – and do it, right now!

Chapter 24

Worship

"So-called worship seems little more than some liturgy (high or low) equated with stained-glass windows, organ music, or emotion-filled songs and prayers. If the bulletin didn't say 'Worship Service,' maybe we wouldn't know what we were supposed to be doing."

(John MacArthur, Jr.)

A.W.Tozer, a man who, if it were not verging on the blasphemous, may be said to have been born before his time, entitled one of his booklets: "Worship: the missing jewel of the evangelical church." Prior to his death, in 1963, he further expressed the opinion that "worship acceptable to God is the missing crown jewel in evangelical Christianity"

Worship. A vast subject; one that fills eternity itself. But there's nothing wrong with big subjects, so worship is the subject at which we look in this chapter.

We may begin by asking the question, "What is worship?" I recall Rev George B. Duncan, as he was preparing me for my forthcoming marriage service, during which I would promise to worship my bride with my body, reminding me that the word comes from an Olde English term that meant "worth-ship". In other words, when we worship, we are expressing the worth that the object of our worship has for us.

Worship is, of course, a very human characteristic. In the most primitive of tribes, animism is practised, and this involves the worship of the spirits of trees, and rocks; of fire and water. One wonders just how far mankind has moved on – in spite of what appears to be a general acceptance of the theory of evolution! - when one sees modern sophisticated man do something very similar, as he worships his car, his golf clubs, his foreign holidays.

It was the Early Church father, Augustine, who is credited with having made the statement, "Thou hast made us for Thyself, and our hearts are restless until they find their rest in Thee"; while a more modern version of the same sentiment has it that "There's a God-shaped blank in every heart, that only God can fill."

Worship, as we've noted, is showing someone, or something, how much they mean to us. Conversely, failure to worship is an indication of how little they mean to us, however vocal our protestations to the contrary!

> "*Therefore, I urge you, brothers, in view of God's mercy, to offer your bodies as living sacrifices, holy and pleasing to God - this is your spiritual act of worship.*" (Rom.12:1).

And it's that aspect of worship that we deal with here.

So let's look, first of all at the Object of our worship — the One to Whom worship is due.

The traditional (and not all that is traditional is somehow 'bad'! call to worship was, simply, "Let us worship God". He alone is the rightful object of our deepest worship. And this is confirmed throughout Scripture:

In Ex.20:3, the first commandment is given in the form

> "*You shall have no other gods before Me.*"

while, by chap.34, after the building of the Tabernacle, and the renewing of the covenant with the Children of Israel, the Lord's instruction is even more explicit:

> "*Do not worship any other god,...*"

The Psalmist, too, emphasised the pre-eminence of the worship of God. In Ps.95:6 we read,

> "*O come, let us worship and bow down; let us kneel before the Lord, our Maker.*"

Again, in Ps.96:9 is the encouragement to

> "*Worship the Lord in the splendour of His holiness; tremble before Him, all the earth.*"

When we move into the New Testament, the situation is no different. Quoting from the Jewish Scriptures – the Old Testament part of the Christian Bible – Jesus responds to the devil's temptation to gain the kingdoms of the world by worshipping him, with the Deuteronomic command,

> "*You shall worship the Lord, your God, and Him only shall you serve.*" (Lk.4:8).

Again, as recorded by John (4:23), He tells the Samaritan woman at Jacob's Well, that true believers

> "*...will worship the Father in spirit, and in truth.*".

In John's great Revelation of the Lord Jesus, and in 14:6-7, the angel proclaims,

> *"Fear God and give Him glory, because the hour of His judgment has come. Worship Him who made the heavens, the earth, the sea and the springs of water."*

while, in 19:10, the direct command of the angel, when John fell at his feet to worship him, is

> *"Worship God!"*

So, Biblically speaking, the only valid object of our worship is to be God Himself – Him and no-one, or nothing, else.

But why worship God? Well, remembering what we've already noticed about the meaning of the word 'worship', our doing so shows the real value we put on him, and the genuine love we have for Him. It shows it to Him.

The vision of God that Jesus has given us, should command all the love and adoration of our hearts, and minds – and pockets! We worship God in the tithes and offerings that we bring to Him. What we give, of our time, our talents, and our material wealth, shows extent, reality, of our love. And I believe that, in some way that I don't even pretend to understand, even the all-mighty, all-knowing, Creator of the universe, needs to see our expression of love; needs to receive our worship. He is not some distant, disinterested, deity, but the One who created us in order that He might have a living, loving relationship with us.

And our worship shows what He means to us, to others.

You see, your very coming out of your home to attend a worship service, is a form of witness. Others do notice. I recall an occasion, many years ago, when my next-door-neighbour and I required to attend to some repairs on the roof of adjoining extensions – built long before either of us had taken possession of our respective dwelling-places. We set aside a couple of days but, as is so often the case, the job proved to be rather more complicated than either of us had anticipated!

The upshot of that was that we were still working on the Sunday afternoon. The Fellowship which my wife and I attended at that time had their main worship service in the evening. At about 5.00 p.m., my neighbour casually mentioned that he assumed that I would be leaving him to finish the job, as I would be "going to church"! I assured him that I would be doing no such thing (believing that it was a better witness to help him to the end!) – but what surprised me was that he had even noticed that we 'went to church' with such regularity!

And, of course, the open door of a church building, with people entering, is a witness. And the greater the number of folk seen to be entering, the more effective the witness.

The Object of our Worship – the Almighty, Triune God; the Creator, and Sustainer of the universe; He, whose very nature is unconditional, immeasurable, Love. He is the Object of our Worship. But we should also consider the manner of our worship.

And if the first point deals with the "Who?, and the Why?" of worship, then this point deals with the "How?"

The simple answer is, "By all that we think, and say, and do." And we may do so in fellowship with one another

> "*Let the word of Christ dwell in you richly as you teach and admonish one another with all wisdom, and as you sing psalms, hymns and spiritual songs with gratitude in your hearts to God.*" (Col.3:16)
>
> "… *as you sing psalms, hymns and spiritual songs with gratitude in your hearts to God.*"

It was Charles Hadden Spurgeon, that great Baptist preacher of a former generation, who said that, "It is said that it is always a token of revival, when there is a revival of psalmody. When Luther's preaching began to tell upon men, you could hear ploughmen at the plough, singing Luther's psalms. Whitefield and Wesley had never done the great work they did, if it had not been for the Charles Wesley's poetry, or for the singing of such men as Toplady, Scott, Newton, and others of the same class. When your heart is full of Christ, you want to sing."

"When your heart is full of Christ, you want to sing.", and even if you aren't a particularly good singer, praise God, you can always take the Psalmist's advice, and

> "...*make a joyful noise to the Lord.*" (Ps.95:1-2)

William Barclay makes the valid point that "It is a counterfeit Christianity that brings an atmosphere of gloom; the real thing radiates joy wherever it comes." Yet how often those who have the opportunity to stand in front of gathered believers, see a total contradiction between the words that are being sung, and the faces of those who are singing! "I've got that joy, joy, joy, joy, down in my heart", as some of us used to sing; but it hasn't always managed to reach my face!!

Now that doesn't mean constantly running around with Cheshire Cat-like grins on our faces. But there should be evidence of a joy that nothing that the world can throw at us can destroy.

> "... *the joy of YHWH is your strength.*",

said Nehemiah to the Jews who had returned to Jerusalem to rebuild the Temple while, centuries later, Paul wrote to the Christians in Ephesus,

"In Him (Jesus) *we were also chosen, having been predestined according to the plan of Him* (the Father) *Who works out everything in conformity with the purpose of His will, in order that we, who were the first to hope in Christ, might be for the praise of His glory."* (1:11-12).

This is the purpose and meaning of life itself. Like many of my generation, I was brought up on the Shorter Catechism. I don't recall every word of it, but I could never forget the first question: "What is the chief end [*prime purpose*] of man?" And the answer given is that "Man's chief end [*prime purpose*] is to glorify God, and to enjoy Him forever." That's my *raison d'être*; that's the reason for my very existence; that's why I live, and move, and have being – that I might bring glory to Him, and enjoy His Presence, eternally!

For many years, I have taken a deep interest in what is generally referred to as the Persecuted Church – those disciples of Jesus who, in the 21st century AD, continue to suffer, and die, for the Name of the Saviour. And a major part of the strength of the Persecuted Church is joy in the face of that persecution.

We worship in fellowship with each other, and we worship in the world.

Worship should be a constant attitude; not confined to an hour or so, twice, or once, on Sunday, with an occasional midweek evening thrown in as a bonus for the Almighty! "The Bible does not view the worship of God as a passing activity on which a person spends a few hours one day a week. Rather, it shows the worship of God to be a full-time responsibility, a work requiring dedication and discipline. God calls upon each of us to be 'a worker who does not need to be ashamed' (II Tim.2:15)." (John W. Ritenbaugh; *Sin, Christians, and the Fear of God*).

In A.W.Tozer's posthumously-published book *Whatever happened to worship?* (also based on a series of preached sermons), he writes "...Monday morning comes... The Christian layman goes to his office. The Christian school teacher goes to the classroom. The Christian mother is busy with duties in the home. [but] If you cannot worship the Lord in the midst of your responsibilities on Monday, it is not very likely that you were worshipping on Sunday!" (p.97)

> "... be [constantly] *filled with the Spirit.*" *writes Paul "Speak to one another with psalms, hymns and spiritual songs. Sing and make music in your heart to the Lord always giving thanks to God the Father for everything, in the Name of our Lord Jesus Christ.*" (Eph.5:18[(b)]-20).

Some of us are good at giving thanks when everything is going our way; when the sun is shining, the birds singing, and life is a totally positive experience! But let the negativity appear; let difficulty line the pathway of life; let one thing after another get in the way of what we want – and it can be a totally different story.

In the book *The Hiding Place*, Corrie ten Boom tells of an experience in the WWII Prisoner of War (Extermination) camp at Ravensbruck, where Corrie managed to conceal a Bible and some vitamin drops for her sister, Betsie. After having spent more than a week in the quarantine compound, she and Betsie were among those moved to permanent quarters, in Barracks 28. They were directed to their "bunks" – straw-covered platforms. Corrie records: "Suddenly I sat up, striking my head on the cross-slat above. Something had pinched my leg.

'Fleas!' I cried. 'Betsie, the place is swarming with them!'

We scrambled across the intervening platforms, heads low to avoid another bump, dropped down to the aisle, and edged our way to a patch of light.

'Here! And here another one!' I wailed. 'Betsie, how can we live in such a place?!'

'Show us. Show us how.' It was said so matter of factly it took me a second to realise she was praying. More and more the distinction between prayer and the rest of life seemed to be vanishing for Betsie.

'Corrie!' she said excitedly. 'He's given us the answer! Before we asked, as He always does! In the Bible this morning. Where was it? Read that part again!'

I glanced down the long dim aisle to make sure no guard was in sight, then drew the Bible from its pouch." (Hodder and Stoughton & CLC, 1971, pps.184-185).

The passage to which Betsie referred was I Thessalonians 5:14ff. Betsie was particularly interested in v.18

> "*give thanks in all circumstances; for this is the will of God in Christ Jesus for you.*"

"'That's it, Corrie! That's His answer. 'Give thanks in all circumstances!' That's what we can do. We can start right now to thank God for every single thing about this new barracks!'"

And so Betsie started – thanking God that she and Corrie were still together; that there had not been an inspection on their arrival, and that they still had their Bible; for the many women who would be sharing the barracks with them who would have the opportunity to hear about the Lord Jesus. Then she continued:

"'Thank You,' Betsie went on serenely, 'for the fleas and for – '

The fleas! This was too much. 'Betsie, there's no way even God can make me grateful for a flea.'

'Give thanks in **all** circumstances,' she quoted. 'It doesn't say, 'in pleasant circumstances'. Fleas are part of this place where God has put us.'

And so we stood between tiers of bunks and gave thanks for fleas. But this time I was sure Betsie was wrong." (op cit, p.185).

Later, the two sisters found themselves able to conduct worship services for the women in the barracks. What surprised them was that no guard ever came near them. Everywhere else, they were always present – but not in Barracks 28! The guards didn't want fleas!!

Giving thanks – always; Praising God – always; Worshipping – always.

All of this is, of course, a form of witness. Others see, by our very attitude, that we are different; set apart; holy. The language we use; the standards by which we live, and work; the way in which we use our time; our money; our material goods. I always find it interesting that while it is the gift and calling of God the Holy Spirit, to be an evangelist (see Eph.4:11; II Tim.4:5), Jesus was speaking to the whole church, in every age, when He said to those original disciples that

> "... *you shall be My **witnesses** in Jerusalem and in all Judea and Samaria and to the end of the earth.*" (Acts 1:8 – *emphasis added*).

> "*Therefore, I urge you, brothers, in view of God's mercy, to offer your bodies as living sacrifices, holy and pleasing to*

God - this is your spiritual act of worship. Do not conform any longer to the pattern of this world, but be transformed by the renewing of your mind. Then you will be able to test and approve what God's will is - His good, pleasing and perfect will. " (Rom.12:1-2).

"Christ has no hands, but our hands to do His work, today.
He has no feet, but our feet, to lead men in His way.
He has no tongues, but our tongues, to tell men how He died.
He has no help, but our help, to bring them to His side.

We are the only Bible the careless world will read.
We are the sinner's Gospel; we are the scoffer's creed.
We are the Lord's last message, given in deed, and word.
What if the type is crooked? What if the print is blurred?

What if our hands are busy with other work than His?
What if our feet are walking where sin's allurement is?
What if our tongues are speaking of things His lips would spurn?
How can we hope to help Him and hasten His return?"

(Annie Johnson Flint)

My whole life; your whole life; ought to be one of praise to God – and, as such, is worship. The Object of our worship; the manner of our worship; and then we must consider the result of our worship

What should be the outcome of our worship? To what end should we engage in this activity?

Within the Godhead there is fellowship between the Father, the Son, and the Holy Spirit. And God created mankind to have fellowship with Him – that man might "… enjoy Him for ever." Sin broke that fellowship.

We see this at the very beginning of the human race. Adam, and Eve, that first created couple, were disobedient to the one command that forbade them something. And in so being, they allowed sin to gain an entry into the perfection that was a garden, *"in Eden, in the east"* (Gen.2:8; NLT). Their own feeble attempt to cover their bodies (3:7[b]) was nothing to do with nakedness/nudity – the "natural" state of mankind (2:25). It was, rather, to do with attempting to cover up their sin; it was a symbol of their unwillingness to confess, and receive the gracious forgiveness of a loving Father God. (see I John 1:9). The close fellowship that they had enjoyed with their Creator, as implied in Gen.3:8, was destroyed – by sin. By the way, this also led to the very first blood-sacrifice, as the Lord provided them with clothing made from animal skins (3:21), which required the death of at least one – and probably more than one – animal. From the very beginning, we may say, sin results in the shedding of blood (see Heb.9:22).

Later, in the history of the Jewish people, the Lord designed a Tabernacle (literally "Tent"), and then a Temple in which they could worship, and offer their own sacrifices for their sins. However, central to both tabernacle and temple was a great veil or curtain that separated the Holy of Holies, in which was the Ark of the Covenant and the Mercy Seat, from the Holy Place. Into the Holy of Holies only the High Priest was allowed – and this on only one day of the year (the Day of Atonement – see ch.6), and after special ablutions (ceremonial washing), and the wearing of special clothing! The veil of the Temple or, later, the memory of it, was the constant reminder to the people of Israel, that the fellowship between the Creator God and the people whom He had created, after His own image, was broken.

In Jesus, that fellowship was restored – for those who put their trust in Him. When He gave up His Spirit, the veil of the Temple was torn in two, from top to bottom. The way was made open again.

> *"Therefore, brothers, since we have confidence to enter the Most Holy Place by the blood of Jesus, by a new and living way opened for us through the curtain, that is, His body, and since we have a great priest over the house of God, let us draw near to God with a sincere heart in full assurance of faith, having our hearts sprinkled to cleanse us from a guilty conscience and having our bodies washed with pure water. Let us hold unswervingly to the hope we profess, for He Who promised is faithful. And let us consider how we may spur one another on towards love and good deeds. Let us not give up meeting together, as some are in the habit of doing, but let us encourage one another - and all the more as you see the Day approaching."* (Heb.10:19-25)

In worship, disciples of Jesus enjoy this restored fellowship with each other.

Showing our love for Him – together;

Bringing our praise to Him – together;

Sharing our life in Him – together.

> *"How good and pleasant it is when brothers live together in unity!"* (Ps.133:1).

And note the promise in v.3:

> *"... for there, YHWH bestows His blessing, even life for evermore"*.

We might compare Gal.3:27-28:

> *"... for all of you who were baptised into Christ have clothed yourselves with Christ. There is neither Jew nor Greek, slave nor free, male nor female, for you are **all one in Christ Jesus**."* (*emphasis added*).

"… all one in Christ Jesus."

We enjoy fellowship with each other; and we enjoy fellowship with the risen Christ.

It's as we worship that we find ourselves drawn, ever closer, to the Object of our love and devotion. It's as we worship that He reveals more and more of Himself to us. It's as we worship that the Holy Spirit softens our hearts and draws us within the veil.

The older I get, the more I change my view of what glory will be like. But one thing certain, for it's clear in Scripture, is that we will worship there as we cannot worship here. But let's get in as much practice here as we possibly can, worshipping Him Who alone is worthy of our love, our obedience, our praise, and our worship.

Chapter 25

ETERNITY

"When I look at Thy heavens, the work of Thy fingers, the moon and the stars which Thou hast established; what is man that Thou art mindful of him, and the son of man that Thou dost care for him?" (Ps 8:3-4)

The final chapter of this book is one that looks at a subject upon which, I freely confess, I have never preached! Indeed, it is not a great word specific to the Christian faith – although the Christian faith teaches that Eternity is the domain of Almighty God.

It is, in a sense, a matter of cosmology, and quantum mechanics – neither of which is a subject in which I hold any formal qualifications! They are subjects, however, in which I have, for many years, taken more than a passing interest. Cosmology is, basically, the study of the known universe – the planets, and stars, and galaxies that we see with our most powerful telescopes. Quantum mechanics has to do with the idea that energy and matter are not continuous but come in small, discrete packets: quanta. Quotations from two famous physicists, gleaned at some time in the recent past, but with no note made of the source(s), sum up its weirdness and complexity – "If quantum mechanics hasn't profoundly shocked you, you haven't understood it." (Niels Bohr); and "I think I can safely say that nobody understands quantum mechanics." (Richard Feynman). Suddenly, the understanding of theology seems like a piece of cake!

I have touched upon this topic, almost *en passant*, in chapter 15 where we looked at predestination. In this chapter, I hope to expand on that, and help you to grasp something of the relationship between time and eternity. It is my contention that, if we manage to grasp even a miniscule fraction of what eternity is, then not only will some of the perceived 'problems' of the Christian faith disappear, but we will also be thrilled and encouraged, and truly be able to say, with Paul

> "*My desire is to depart and be with Christ, for that is far better.*" (Phil.1:23).

One author has written, "There can be no worthier object of mental application than the eternal God and His relation to eternity and time. ... Churches today are filled with ... critics who have more concern for time than for eternity. They do not know that the greater knowledge believers have of eternal verities the better equipped they are to redeem the time." (W.E.Best; *Eternity and Time*; South Belt Grace Church, 1986; pps.1-2). If this chapter should enable someone to grasp that fraction already mentioned, it will be worthwhile – as, indeed, it will be even if it does no more than encourage a deeper study of this amazing subject!

The first thing that we need to realise is that time is a created entity, with a beginning and, ultimately, an end; and that eternity is not "endless time". The reality, a reality that helps to answer so many of the apparently difficult questions about the faith, is that eternity is a dimension that is outwith, separate from, yet containing, time. It is, more correctly, "timelessness".

Let me try to explain this concept of dimensions. Many of us, in school, learned that "a straight line is the shortest distance between two points". What may not have been explained was that such a line can only be notional, i.e. I may imagine it, but I am unable to reproduce it in any tangible form! As soon as I put pencil (or any other marking implement) to paper (or any other medium) and join those two points, I produce something that has three dimensions: length, breadth, and height. It is true that, if I use a very fine point to draw my line, the breadth and height will be barely noticeable to the naked eye. But they will exist, and will be measurable by highly-sophisticated instruments.

Even a two-dimensional object, like a rectangle, with obvious length and breadth, cannot be produced in a tangible form without the addition of height – the height of the ink, or whatever, above the medium on which the drawing is made.

We live in a physically three-dimensional universe, in which every "solid" object has length, breadth, and height. However, there is a fourth dimension that is common to us all. That is the dimension of time – time that is measurable in days, hours, minutes, etc.

Modern physicists inform us that there may be as many as eleven, or even twelve, dimensions in the known universe. Prof Stephen Hawking is one who would maintain that two of these dimensions are 'time' dimensions. There is the one in which we live, and which he illustrates graphically as a straight line with its past, present, and future. The second 'time' dimension, he suggests, crosses that straight line, but touches it at every point while being separate from it! I recall reading this for the first time and thinking: "He's describing eternity!" (see *The Universe in a Nutshell, pps.59ff*).

When it comes to timelessness, most of us are, in fact, somewhat familiar with the concept. The way in which I most easily think of it is by going back in my memory (which is, of course, time-bound!) to the days when I was 'courting' the young girl who eventually became my wife. As our relationship grew, and we became more serious about spending our lives with one another, we would often sit, in the evening, in the front room of her parental home, discussing our future together – where I might be called to minister (I was already at University studying for that vocation); how many children we might have; whether or not we would have a dog; and her insistence that she was not going to become this character who was "the minister's wife", but rather the wife of a man who happened to be a minister! Suddenly, I would look up at the clock on the wall above the fireplace. "Look at the time!", I might exclaim. "I'd better go before your dad comes in and throws me out!" What had happened was, that for an all-too-brief interlude, time for us had effectively ceased to exist. We had been so engrossed in ourselves, and our plans, that we had forgotten about it. Of course, the clock on the wall had not been so distracted! And so, when I saw the position of its hands, I was brought sharply back to the reality of my time-bound existence.

And that is the 'problem' with time. It carries us powerfully along with itself from the "no longer" (the past), to the "not yet" (the future). There is no opportunity, or possibility, of "turning back the hands of time"; no stopping it, however agreeable the present moment that we experience.

Eternity is different!

Within time, one cannot speak of either the past or the future having any reality. Both are merely conceptual (i.e., we may imagine them, from the point of view of memory or anticipation, respectively) but we are unable to experience them. Only the present has reality, and eternity may be expressed as "the immeasurable present". This, I realised many years ago, is why when Moses asked for the Name of the One Who spoke from a burning bush, he was told:

"I AM WHO I AM" (Ex 3:14).

If YHWH had stated "I was", that would have indicated changeableness – He is not, now, what He once was. On the other hand, if He had said "I will be", that would suggest that He is not yet what He is to become! The very Name by which the Creator revealed Himself is evidence of the "abiding presentness" of eternity. In eternity, there is no past; there is no future; all is NOW! It is today without yesterday or tomorrow; existence without bounds or dimensions; duration without beginning or end.

And there is a difference in quality. W.E. Best writes: "There is a difference between the succession of events in time, and the intensity of experience in eternity. Intensity of experience will replace extensity when time ceases to exist. The word extensity means the quality of having extension. Psychologically, it is the attitude or sensation by which spatial (pertaining to space which also involves time) extension is perceived. The word intensity refers to the quality or condition of being intense. The essential quality of eternity is intensity rather than extensity. For example, to think of length as the essence [essential quality] of eternal life is to suppose that the reality of it is to be measured by how long it lasts. We are so conscious of our mortality that we tend to emphasise the quantative aspect of our life in Christ, with its guarantee of victory over death. However, the qualitative aspect of our life in Christ is immensely significant." (*op cit*, p.10). That's why the more accurate translations of John 3:16 – the Gospel in a nutshell – end with the words "... *eternal life*", rather than "... *everlasting life.*" The new life that is received when one is truly born again of the Spirit of God is not just one of immeasurably greater duration, but of immeasurably greater quality. It is, indeed, the life of Eternal God being lived through the believer!

So what will we experience in eternity? First of all, that depend on where we are! Heaven and hell are often closely associated with eternity, and it is a simple fact that Jesus spoke more often about hell than He did about heaven. However, if we wish to spend eternity in heaven – in that dimension of perfect bliss where, we are assured,

> "... *the dwelling of God is with men. He will dwell with them, and they shall be His people, and God Himself will be with them; He will wipe away every tear from their eyes and death shall be no more, neither shall there be mourning nor crying nor pain any more, for the former things have passed away."* (Rev. 21:3-4),

then we must be born again (Jn.3:16), as already referred to in chap 3. Failure to respond, positively and personally, to the offer of salvation – purchased at such great cost – means that eternity is spent with the devil and his angels, in hell, in

> "... *the unquenchable fire.*" (Mark 9:43).

However, for those who choose real life now, there is an experience that is beyond our mortal comprehension. Let us consider the 'journey' there! Sometimes one is given the impression that heaven is "away up there", a trillion light-years away! So even that great servant of God of a former generation, John Bunyan, writes "And before I was aware, I found myself far above the earth, which seemed to me a very small point in comparison with that region of lights into which I was translated. ... ... I then said, 'I would fain be informed what that dark spot, so far below me, is which has grown less and less as I have mounted higher and higher, and appears much darker since I have come into this region of light'." (*Vision of Heaven and Hell*; Gospel Publishing House, Springfield Missouri; pps.10-11).

Now I would emphasise that heaven is a real, physical, place. Jesus assures us that:

> *"In my Father's house are many rooms; if it were not so, would I have told you that I go to prepare a place for you? And when I go and prepare a place for you, I will come again and will take you to Myself, that where I am you may be also."* (John 14:2-3).

But it is close! I recently learned of a material called graphene which, I am assured, is only one atom in thickness. That means that, by comparison, the finest conceivable gossamer is like extra-heavy brocade! I believe, firmly, that what separates time from eternity is finer than graphene, yet of a strength that even if every nuclear device possessed by mankind was to detonate simultaneously, there would not be even the slightest dent in, or the faintest scratch on, that veil.

And eternity is full of praise and worship. In the Revelation given to John, we read that he looked and

> *"... heard around the throne and the living creatures and the elders the voice of many angels, numbering myriads of myriads and thousands of thousands, saying with a loud voice, 'Worthy is the Lamb Who was slain, to receive power and wealth and wisdom and might and honour and glory and blessing!' And I heard every creature in heaven and on earth and under the earth and in the sea, and all therein, saying, 'To Him Who sits upon the throne and to the Lamb be blessing and honour and glory and might for ever and ever!' And the four living creatures said, 'Amen!' and the elders fell down and worshipped."* (Rev.5:11-14).

> *"And the twenty-four elders and the four living creatures fell down and worshipped God Who is seated on the*

> *throne, saying, 'Amen. Hallelujah!' And from the throne came a voice crying,*
>
> *'Praise our God, all you His servants,*
> *you who fear Him, small and great.'*
>
> *Then I heard what seemed to be the voice of a great multitude, like the sound of many waters and like the sound of mighty thunderpeals, crying,*
>
> *'Hallelujah! For the Lord our God the Almighty reigns.*
> *Let us rejoice and exult and give Him the glory,*
> *for the marriage of the Lamb has come,*
> *and His Bride has made herself ready;*
> *it was granted her to be clothed with fine linen, bright and pure'*
> *– for the fine linen is the righteous deeds of the saints."*
> (Rev.19:4-8)

Heaven is, in Biblical teaching, the dwelling-place of Almighty God, where – with one brief episode of silence (and that does not, of itself, preclude worship which, as many of us can testify to in even our mortal lives, does not always have to be vocal and audible) – He is worshipped, continuously, in His Triune Being.

So what happens at the moment of physical death? Well, for the disciple of Jesus, the answer is simple. Paul tells us, in II Cor.5:8 that to be absent from the body is to be present with the Lord. Jesus, Himself assured the repentant thief on the cross that

> "... *today you will be with Me in Paradise.*" (Luke 23:43).

So it doesn't seem to be the case that, when I die – and this is, of course, only applicable for as long as the rapture of the saints of God is delayed – I travel millions of light years to reach my celestial abode! No, it's as instantaneous as it will be at the rapture when, Paul tells us,

> "*It will happen in a moment, in the blink of an eye, when the last trumpet* [shofar] *is blown.*" (I Cor.15:52).

We find further hints of this when we look in the O.T. Remember the great old patriarch, Enoch? I love those words recorded of him in Gen.5:23-24 –

> "*Enoch lived 365 years, walking in close fellowship with God. Then one day he disappeared, because God took him.*"

Or, as the older translations put it,

> "*... he was not; for God took him.*" (KJV).

So what happened to Enoch? Well, what I am now going to share is, I confess, totally speculative. But I share it with you because I am convinced, not only of its possibility, but of its probability! I believe that those words are telling us that, every morning, after the birth of Methuselah (Gen.5:22), when Enoch awoke, his first words were "Well, Lord, where are we going today; what will we be doing?" And the Lord told him. Then, one day, he awoke and, having asked the same question, was told by God, "Today, Enoch, dear friend, you are coming to my place. Let's go!" And Enoch simply walked through that ultra-fine veil that separates time from eternity.

Or what about Elijah? Listen to these words from the Second Book of Kings:

> "*When the Lord was about to take Elijah up to heaven in a whirlwind, Elijah and Elisha were travelling from Gilgal. And Elijah said to Elisha, 'Stay here, for the Lord has told*

> *me to go to Bethel.' ... As they were walking along and talking, suddenly a chariot of fire appeared, drawn by horses of fire. It drove between the two men, separating them, and Elijah was carried by a whirlwind into heaven."* (2:1-2,11)

May I suggest that, once again, that veil had been parted, and this mighty servant of YHWH, was taken through to receive his reward?

Returning to the N.T., we go back to the Mount of Transfiguration. Matthew, as we noted earlier, records:

> *"Six days later Jesus took Peter and the two brothers, James and John, and led them up a high mountain to be alone. As the men watched, Jesus' appearance was transformed so that His face shone like the sun, and His clothes became as white as light. Suddenly, Moses and Elijah appeared and began talking with Jesus."* (17:1-3).

What had happened? I believe, firmly, that this veil between time and eternity had been parted; that Moses and Elijah simply stepped through that temporary gateway between here and there.

And how often have we read, or heard, of a true saint of God who, on their deathbed, with face suddenly glowing, seems to be aware of those who have gone before, even of the Saviour Who awaits their homecoming? I believe that the veil has been parted, just a little, for them, and they are being permitted that early vision of the glorious place to which they are about to be taken. It's not a long journey – just a step through the veil.

Sa'id Musa, a Christian employee of the Red Cross in Afghanistan, was arrested in late May, 2010, after footage of Afghan Christians being baptised was shown on national television. Musa, a father of six, and an amputee with a prosthetic leg, was beaten, forcefully deprived of sleep, and sexually abused. Thankfully, he was released in the following February, and granted asylum in a European country.

But on Dec 11th 2010 he wrote, from his prison cell, that he rejoices in the Lord amidst his suffering. "I saw a vision, during my sleep one night, of the heaven opened, and a Person – His clothes like snow, His face in dazzling light – came to me, and put His hand on my shoulder, and said to me 'Please be happy. I am always with you in this jail. I chose you, and you should announce my Good News to the people of Afghanistan and all over the world.' At that moment, I was shaking and trembling with fear. I fell down and could not stand. He took my hands, and I woke up."

So what had this dear brother experienced? Was it all just the result of indigestion? Was he beginning to lose his mind? Or did that veil – that fine, fine, curtain – part slightly to give him that glimpse of the exalted Saviour, strengthening him in his suffering, his torment, his anguish? I know what I believe!

It's a veil through which each of us must ultimately pass. The only question concerns what we find on the other side. For it is only for those who, having recognised their sinfulness, have come to the Saviour in repentance and faith, and accepted the salvation that He won on the cross of Calvary, that the veil leads to the heavenly places. For all others, it leads to a lost eternity, without hope, because it is without Jesus.

May each one of us hear what God would say to us, as individuals, that others may see something of His nature in us; that we may see more of His glory in the face of the Lord Jesus; that we may spend much time in His presence, seeking His will, receiving His blessing, that we might fulfil His purpose; that when our time comes, we might take that final step into His nearer Presence, to hear those wonderful words,

> *"Well done, good and faithful servant. Enter into the joy of your Lord."* (Matt.25:21, *et al*)

– and to dwell there, throughout eternity.

In Conclusion

If any of the topics that have been covered in this book have caused you to consider your own eternal destiny; or if you have discovered, as you have read, that you do not – but would love to – have a living relationship with Almighty God, through the Son, then please feel free to contact the author at

author@minister.com

Further copies of the book may be purchased, as an e-book, from Amazon at

https://www.amazon.co.uk/dp/B009EG6TJW

This volume is the first of a planned series. Further volumes are introduced in the following pages.

Postscript!

If you found this book to be helpful, **PLEASE** leave a positive review on Amazon.

This is because Amazon promotes books based on the number of reviews an individual book receives. No reviews ... the book will remain a secret.

Please remember that I receive **no** financial benefit from the sale of my books. **ALL** royalties are paid, **directly**, into the Bank Account of *Release International*, in support of the persecuted church.

If you are able to also recommend the book – <u>and the others in the series</u> – within your own Christian Fellowship, and among family and friends, encouraging them to purchase, this would be greatly appreciated. Perhaps your Amazon review could be reproduced in any regular newsletter, or the equivalent, that is published in the Fellowship!

Thank you, on behalf of those brothers and sisters who suffer for their faith in the Lord Jesus, in ways that most of us are truly unable to fully imagine, or understand.

About the author.

Brian Ross is an ordained minister of the Gospel, happily married and with two daughters, one of whom is herself married, and who has provided him with a grandson. He holds a number of academic qualifications, from a variety of establishments and in a variety of disciplines.

However, the qualification that is dearest to his heart is his Diploma of the Bible Training Institute – the result of his first foray into tertiary education, and the one that provided him with a solid evangelical base as he proceeded to achieve other academic success.

He has led a varied life, having commenced his adult work as a chef (including two years in the British Merchant Navy in which he was privileged to visit many parts of the world), continued as a parish minister in the Church of Scotland (Presbyterian), and completed it as Head of Religious and Moral Education in a Scottish State Secondary School. He has also been a regular presenter with two Christian radio stations; successfully presented a case at a two-part Industrial Tribunal; and twice stood (unsuccessfully!) as a candidate for the Scottish Christian Party at Holyrood and local elections. He spent the first three years of his 'retirement' as an active Chaplain to Strathclyde Police Force, deployed in 'N', and 'Q', Divisions, and at the Force Training and Recruitment Centre. He now exercises a ministry in south-west France – to both English-speaking and French-speaking groups.

His 'non-commercial' blog (www.crazyrev.blogspot.com) is, basically, a 'ministry blog', and he endeavours to post with a certain regularity! He contributes to various online fora and, of course, preaches whenever, and wherever, he is provided with the opportunity (all invitations prayerfully considered - author@minister.com).

Foundations of the Faith.

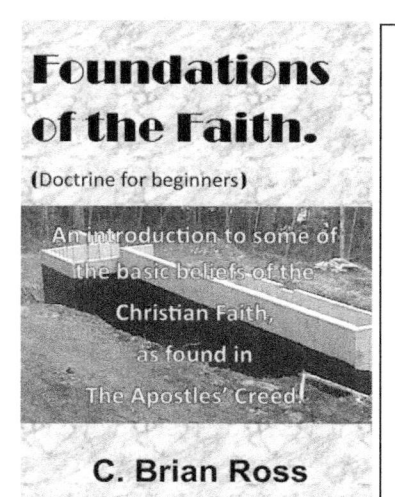

(Doctrine for beginners)

An introduction to some of the basic beliefs of the Christian Faith, as found in The Apostles' Creed.

C. Brian Ross

ALL Royalties go to support the persecuted church.

Getting to know some basic Christian teaching, using the wording of "The Apostles' Creed"

Price (in UK) £8.99

ISBN: 10: 151731206X
ISBN: 13: 978-1517312060

(Kindle e-book also available at £3.99)

Links available at

https://crazyrev.blogspot.com/

Following up his "Great Words of the Faith", this is a timely piece of very accessible writing from a respected and experienced writer, teacher, and preacher. … It is accessible, scholarly, personal, and full of scripture reference. The difficult issues are not skirted, but the fundamental truth of the Godhead is allowed to shine through.

Dr. Ken Cunningham, CBE, FRSA.

"*Foundations of the Faith*" should help all of those seeking to follow the Way of the Christ to do so more faithfully, and in an informed manner.

Rev. Derek Hughes, BSc., BD., DipEd.

Brian articulates what he believes with freshness and clarity. It is clear that for him, as for the distinguished Russian thinker, Berdyaev, Jesus is the starting point for learning Who God is, who we are, and what life is all about.

Very Rev. Dr. James A. Simpson, BSc., BD, STM

Defending the Faith

(Letters from John)

C. Brian Ross

ALL royalties go to support the persecuted church.

A walk through the letters of the apostle, John, as he shows us how to deal with false teaching.

Price (in UK) £8.99

ISBN: 9781791394387

(Kindle e-book also available at £3.99)

Links available at

https://crazyrev.blogspot.com/

"I warmly commend this excellent piece of work from the pen of Brian Ross on the New Testament Letters of John. ... I would expect it to have a wide uptake throughout the Christian church."

Rev. Eric J Alexander
Formerly minister to St George's–Tron Parish Church, Glasgow

"This is a very readable book, and I would happily have it available to hand out to encourage people to understand, more deeply, their need to speak out their faith to those amongst whom they live."

Rev. Dominic Stockford,
Minister, Christ Church, Teddington.
Chairman, The Protestant Truth Society

"Brian Ross ... deals in I John with, among other things, the need for disciples of Jesus to be aware of false teaching ... the importance of fellowship; and the need to grow in the faith. In II John, he draws out the apostle's warning against false, itinerant, teachers while, in the third of the letters, he shows that John commends hospitality, and condemns a spirit of control."

The Venerable Dr Paul Vrolijk
Senior Chaplain and Canon Chancellor
Archdeacon of North West Europe

Printed in Great Britain
by Amazon